Blackstone's Guide to the

PROTECTION FROM HARASSMENT ACT 1997

Blackstone's Guide to the

PROTECTION FROM HARASSMENT ACT 1997

Timothy Lawson-Cruttenden,
TD, MA, Solicitor-Advocate

&

Neil Addison, BA, Barrister

b BLACKSTONE
PRESS LIMITED

First published in Great Britain 1997 by Blackstone Press Limited,
9–15 Aldine Street, London W12 8AW. Telephone 0181-740 2277

© Timothy Lawson-Cruttenden and Neil Addison, 1997

ISBN: 1 85431 695 8

British Library Cataloguing in Publication Data
A CIP catalogue record for this book is available from the British Library.

Typeset by Montage Studios Limited, Tonbridge, Kent
Printed by Ashford Colour Press, Gosport, Hampshire

Contents

1.1 The emergence of the tort of harassment   1.2 The Court of Appeal decision in *Burris* v *Azadani*   1.3 The development of 'offences of harassment' by the Court of Appeal Criminal Division   1.4 Recent developments in the general criminal law concerned with 'offences of harassment'   1.5 High profile acquittals in 1996   1.6 Problems with the existing civil and criminal law   1.7 The significance of the Act   1.8 Progress of the Bill

2.1 Requirements of the offence   2.2 Relevance of civil cases   2.3 Elements of the offence   2.4 Course of conduct   2.5 Other offences   2.6 Choice between harassment and other charges   2.7 Relevance of previous convictions   2.8 Time between incidents   2.9 Harassment of another   2.10 Defining harassment   2.11 Alarm and distress   2.12 Defences to a charge of criminal harassment   2.13 Stalkers   2.14 Effect on journalists   2.15 Protesters   2.16 Noise harassment   2.17 Northern Ireland   2.18 Plea bargaining

3.1 Introduction   3.2 The definition of harassment   3.3 The manner in which the civil courts may consider allegations of harassment   3.4 The definition of victims of harassment   3.5 The definition of alarming or causing distress   3.6 Defence to the civil tort of harassment   3.7 Damages for the statutory tort of harassment   3.8 The practical application of section 3   3.9 Domestic violence   3.10 Protesters   3.11 Hunt saboteurs   3.12 The media   3.13 Neighbourhood disputes   3.14 Northern Ireland

Foreword

As the authors rightly stress, 'harassment goes to the very heart of the issue of conflict in society'. This book will help us all, whether we are lawyer, police officer, magistrate or judge. Academics should welcome it too.

The Act can apply in civil, criminal or family jurisdictions. All these are most competently covered in a practical and realistic way. Furthermore, the authors explore the political background and have not hesitated to mention possible problems, even listing some earlier high profile acquittals. The seven appendices are invaluable.

Timothy Lawson-Cruttenden, a solicitor, was the advocate in the leading case of *Burris* v *Azadani* and has written widely on the subject. Neil Addison, formerly with the Crown Prosecution Service, is a barrister with considerable experience in the criminal courts.

Together, they have produced a book which is both useful and interesting — quite a rare achievement.

H. H. Judge Christopher Compston
Wandsworth County Court
London SW15

Introduction

The purpose of this guide is to describe the effect of the Protection from Harassment Act 1997 ('the Act') and to set it in the context of the present civil and criminal law as they relate to offences of harassment.

Harassment goes to the very heart of the issue of conflict in society. The relevant law is likely to be of concern to all lawyers who practise civil or criminal litigation. Neighbourhood disputes, racial hatred, bullying at work, confrontation with the media, or the protection of celebrities from unwanted attention are all affected. The policing of hunt protesters, industrial strikers or noisy and nuisance tenants are also relevant. All such areas could be the subject of proceedings under the Act. Both civil and criminal lawyers, whether they be media or employment law experts or concerned with racial hatred, neighbourhood disputes or domestic violence, will ignore this Act at their peril.

Though we have dealt separately with the civil and criminal provisions of the Act, both the civil and the criminal law are, unusually, intermingled. Criminal lawyers will find chapter 3 on the civil law of value in defining what 'harassment' is. Civil lawyers will have to consider whether taking out private criminal prosecutions and obtaining a criminal restraining order may be more effective than applying for a civil injunction. A salient factor in making such a determination will be the different burdens of proof which are applied by the civil and criminal courts.

THE AIM OF THE ACT

The main provisions of the Protection from Harassment Act 1997 are summarised as follows:

(a)   Two criminal offences are created, namely the summary offence of criminal harassment (s. 2) and an aggravated indictable offence (s. 4) involving the fear of violence.

(b)   A statutory tort of harassment is created by s. 3 and criminal courts are given the unprecedented jurisdiction to punish the breach of civil court orders. Breach of an injunction made under s. 3 is a criminal offence (s. 3(6)).

(c)   Criminal courts are given the power to make injunction-style restraining orders on convicted defendants prohibiting them from further conduct which might be injurious to the victim (s. 5).

(d)   In addition to creating the two new criminal offences and the new statutory tort, the Act seeks to cure two defects in the civil and criminal law as follows:

(i)   the absence of a power of arrest at common law. The criminal courts are now enabled to enforce civil orders made under s. 3 of the Act; additionally s. 3(3) allows a civil plaintiff to make an *ex parte* application for a warrant for the arrest of the defendant.

(ii)   the inability of criminal courts to order the equivalent of civil injunctions. The restraining orders provided for by s. 5 of the Act are an attempt to remedy this.

The Act itself is short but its ramifications are complex and far-reaching. In this guide we have attempted to follow the layout of the Act itself. Therefore chapter 1 deals with the background to the Act. Chapter 2 deals with the offence of criminal harassment created by the combination of ss. 1 and 2. Chapter 3 covers the civil tort of harassment formed by the combination of ss. 1 and 3. Chapter 4 covers the offence of causing fear of violence created by s. 4. Chapter 5 covers the new restraining orders created by s. 5. In chapter 6, we return to s. 3 and consider the complex, cumbersome and possibly unworkable provisions of the Act regarding breach of civil courts' anti-harassment injunctions.

We are not Scots lawyers and therefore we have not attempted to deal with those sections of the Act which relate to Scotland. However, we have sympathy with those Scottish lawyers who consider that Scots law was dealing perfectly adequately with the problem of harassment in Scotland and that the new Act merely imposes on Scotland an English law solution to an English law problem.

The Act can be extended to cover Northern Ireland by Order in Council made under s. 13. If this is done, the law applying in Northern Ireland will be the same as that applying in England. There are, however, certain uses of the Act which could potentially have a particular relevance to Northern Ireland, and we have referred to these possibilities in the text.

We have provided various Appendices. These list in shorthand form the principles of civil harassment and other criminal offences dealing with harassment. We have also provided sample statements of claim and injunctions, and examples of possible restraining orders. We hope that these will prove of practical value to the busy (indeed harassed!) lawyers, police officers, judges and magistrates whose responsibility it will be to make sense of the new law.

Chapter 1
Background to the Act

1.1 The emergence of the tort of harassment

It is remarkable how quickly the law of harassment has emerged. Even before the Act it was clear that harassment had become a primary tort and was no longer subsumed under the torts of nuisance, trespass or trespass to the person.

This development is all the more remarkable bearing in mind the *dicta* of Sir Peter Gibson J in *Khorasandjian* v *Bush* [1993] 3 All ER 669, CA; although giving a minority judgment, he stated that 'there is no tort of harassment' (p. 683 at H). This echoed the 1992 Law Commission Report in which the Commission stated that it did not wish to create 'something approaching a new tort of harassment or molestation' (Law Com No. 207, para. 3.8).

The reluctance of the Law Commission to support the creation of a new tort of harassment is borne out by the following:

> We do not think it is appropriate that this jurisdiction [the proposed family law non-molestation order] should be available to resolve issues such as disputes between neighbours, harassment of tenants by landlords or cases of sexual harassment in the workplace. Here there is no domestic or family relationship to justify special remedies or procedures and resort should properly be had to the remedies provided under property and employment law. (Law Com No. 207, para. 3.14)

1.2 The Court of Appeal decision in *Burris* v *Azadani*

The tort of harassment finally emerged in *Burris* v *Azadani* [1995] 4 All ER 802, CA, on 27 July 1995. The lead judgment is that of Sir Thomas Bingham MR (as he then was), his *dicta* being as follows:

(a) '... nor, in the light of ... [previous] ... authority, can the view be upheld that there is no tort of harassment' (p. 809 at B);

(b) 'Ordinarily the victim will be adequately protected by an injunction which restrains the tort which has been or is likely to be committed, whether trespass to the person or to land, interference with goods, harassment, intimidation or as the case may be' (at p. 811).

Six principles emerged from this judgment. These are fundamental to a consideration of both the new statutory tort of harassment and the criminal offence of harassment, and are set out in Appendix 2. To a considerable extent they reveal the different way in which civil courts and criminal courts approach the problem of harassment.

Civil courts are concerned primarily with the protection of the victim and with the imposition of injunctive relief. Interlocutory injunctions can be ordered on the establishment of an arguable cause of action and will be imposed 'where it appears to the court to be just and convenient' (Supreme Court Act 1981, s. 37(1)). It is submitted that a plaintiff applying for an interlocutory injunction need satisfy a relatively low evidential test (on the civil burden of proof, namely on a balance of probabilities), although it is clear that the interests of justice are paramount. Civil courts have power to restrain what would otherwise be lawful behaviour. Civil relief is awarded by balancing the interests and obligations of the respective parties. Thus the civil courts will adopt a pragmatic and commonsense approach to the issue of harassment. Such an approach may be neither legalistic nor founded on conventional causes of action.

Criminal courts, however, only have power to convict for behaviour which is unlawful. While the rights of the victim are relevant, criminal courts are primarily concerned with sentencing the convicted offender. Consequently, if the criminal burden of proof is not discharged a defendant might escape scot-free in circumstances where a civil court would have imposed stringent injunctive terms. Consequently criminal law delivers 'conviction or nothing'.

1.3 The development of 'offences of harassment' by the Court of Appeal Criminal Division

Rapid developments in the criminal law relating to harassment took place in the summer of 1996. The decision in *R* v *Burstow* (1996) *The Times*, 30 July, established the doctrine of psychological assault. This enables a defendant to be convicted of assault even though he or she may not have applied direct physical force. Consequently these offences can take in campaigns of non-physical harassment provided that such campaigns cause psychiatric or psychological harm and impair a victim's health accordingly.

In *R* v *Ireland* (1996) *The Times*, 22 May, it was held that a threatening telephone call or series of calls can constitute assault. Such calls have to place their victims in immediate fear for their safety, with resulting psychological or psychiatric injury.

In *R* v *Johnston* (1996) *The Times*, 22 May, it was held that hundreds of obscene telephone calls to at least 13 different women in the south Cumbria area was conduct which constituted a public nuisance.

The importance of these decisions in relation to the general law of harassment cannot be overstated. The classic harasser often conducts a campaign of 'passive' harassment seeking to ensure that he or she does not commit an overt act which might constitute an offence. Many of the ingredients of harassment involve misuse of telephone calls. Consequently, the extension of the doctrine of assault to such behaviour — combined with the doctrine of criminal public nuisance — was significant although academically controversial. Many lawyers considered that the meaning of 'assault' was being extended in a wholly artificial way. Since the Act does not affect the existing law, these cases are still good law and similar prosecutions can still be mounted under them. For this reason the cases are summarised in Appendix 3.

1.4   Recent developments in the general criminal law concerned with 'offences of harassment'

In addition to the doctrines of psychological assault, telephone assault and criminal public nuisance, three other offences dealing with 'harassment-type behaviour' are particularly significant: intentional harassment, obscene letters and parcels, and malicious telephone calls:

(a)   The offence of intentional harassment was created by s. 154 of the Criminal Justice and Public Order Act 1994, and now forms s. 4A of the Public Order Act 1986 (see Appendix 4). In order to secure a conviction for intentional harassment, the prosecution have to prove subjective intention on the part of the defendant. This has caused numerous difficulties because many alleged harassers are able to establish that they did not intend to harass. For example, some defendants infatuated with a particular person have argued that they are the victims of unrequited love and therefore not guilty of intentionally harassing.

In his speech introducing the Protection from Harassment Bill to the House of Commons on 17 December 1996, Michael Howard said: '... we have not defined harassment itself. Harassment as a concept has been interpreted regularly by the courts since 1986'. Some 100 prosecutions under s. 4A were successful in 1995 (Hansard, 17 December 1996, col. 784).

The failure of this offence was an important contributing factor in the Government's decision to bring in the 1997 Act. The principal difference in the Act is that intention does not have to be proved, and instead harassment is considered from the point of view of the reasonable person.

(b)   The offence of sending obscene letters or parcels was created by s. 1(1) of the Malicious Communications Act 1988. As many harassers indulge in sending obscene letters or parcels containing offensive material, this section is an important part of the prosecution armoury and may form an alternative to a charge of harassment under the 1997 Act.

(c)   The offence of making malicious telephone calls was created by s. 43(1) of the Telecommunications Act 1984. Telephone calls which do not constitute assault or criminal public nuisance may be malicious, thereby grounding a charge under this section. The offence was originally punishable only with a fine, but the maximum penalty was raised to six months' imprisonment by s. 92 of the Criminal Justice and Public Order Act 1994.

The ordinary offences of harassment cannot now be viewed independently either of the general common law or of the existing criminal law. The Act has been drafted in the light of recent developments in the criminal law, most of which are set out in Appendix 3.

Lawyers considering the offences of harassment should also consider offences concerned with criminal damage and excessive noise. All the relevant statutory offences involving harassment or fear are set out in Appendix 4.

1.5   High profile acquittals in 1996

There were four significant acquittals in 1996, and a discussion of these cases formed part of the debate in Parliament when the Bill was being considered. These acquittals revealed some of the weaknesses in the existing criminal law which the Act seeks to remedy. They are as follows:

(a)   In January 1996, Bernard Quinn was found not guilty of behaviour likely to cause a breach of the peace when he attempted to break through a security cordon placed around the Princess Royal. The decision was made by a stipendiary magistrate at Liverpool, who clearly took the view that peaceful attempts to breach a security cordon did not constitute an offence. It is significant that Quinn was not bound over to keep the peace despite the fact that he had a strong reputation for being an infatuated 'stalker' of the Princess Royal to whom he had written hundreds of letters and in respect of whom he apparently indulged in sexual fantasies.

(b)   In March 1996, Dr Klaus Wagner was found not guilty of similar behaviour and again was not bound over. He was a compulsive 'stalker' of both the Queen and Diana, Princess of Wales. On the occasion in question, he was holding a placard outside Buckingham Palace bearing the words 'The Queen is the Devil'. Video footage made it clear that the crowd around him acted peacefully and entirely ignored him. Consequently his behaviour, however distasteful, was not likely to cause a breach of the peace. On the contrary, it provoked no response whatsoever.

Much time was spent in Parliament debating whether any changes in the law were needed, and it was suggested that charges of breach of the peace and bind over orders were sufficient to deal with harassers. The acquittals of Quinn and Wagner made it clear, however, that the law on breach of the peace was inadequate; and even if binding over orders had been made, breach of such an order is punishable only with a fine which would not constitute any form of deterrent to a determined stalker.

(c)   In March 1996, Wilson was found not guilty of intentional harassment by Horseferry Road magistrates' court, despite the fact that he had perpetrated a course of infatuated behaviour against Charlotte Sell for many years.

(d) In September 1996, Chambers was found not guilty of psychological assault despite the fact that his campaign of harassment against Margaret Bent involved, on one occasion, threatening her with a knife. He had constantly 'stalked' her. He telephoned her up to ten times a day. He had sat outside her house with a machete. He had registered his car in her name and ensured that she received a string of parking tickets, followed by summonses and writs by bailiffs threatening to seize her property if fines were unpaid. The judge ruled that there was insufficient evidence to prove intention, on Chambers' part, to cause psychological harm. It is not clear why the judge did not allow the case to proceed on the charge of 'simple' GBH (Offences Against the Persons Act 1861, s. 20) which does not require evidence of intent.

The acquittal of Chambers reveals the deficiencies in the restraining orders provided by s. 5 of the Act which can take effect only on conviction. It is the opinion of the authors that any civil court hearing these facts would have imposed stringent injunctive terms on Chambers ordering him not to have any further contact with Margaret Bent.

A summary of these high profile acquittals is set out at Appendix 3.

1.6   Problems with the existing civil and criminal law

The Act seeks to remedy the absence of a power of arrest at common law and the inability of criminal courts to order the equivalent of civil injunctions. Solutions to these defects are offered only in relation to harassment as defined and provided for by the Act. Consequently the existing problems must not be ignored because practitioners will be concerned with them when considering alternative criminal offences or alternative torts. It is the opinion of the authors that civil defendants who wish to avoid being charged with breaching civil orders may offer undertakings which are not injunctions for the purposes of s. 3(6) of the Act, and therefore breach of them would not constitute a criminal offence. Alternatively, defendants might offer injunctions under other torts — whether nuisance, trespass to the person or trespass — and thereby once again avoid the provisions of s. 3(6).

Similarly criminal practitioners may be concerned with avoiding the jurisdiction of the criminal courts to make restraining orders under the Act, and may therefore seek to offer pleas to the alternative offences set out in Appendix 4 in respect of which restraining orders cannot be made.

1.7   The significance of the Act

The Government appears to have a low expectation of the significance of the Act. The explanatory memorandum to the Bill stated '... it is anticipated that approximately 200 extra criminal cases a year will arise in ... [the criminal] jurisdiction, resulting in additional costs to the Courts, the Crown Prosecution Service and Legal Aid of £216,000 per annum. ...'.

We do not share the Government's low expectations. In our view, thousands of people perpetrate harassment each year or consider that they are victims of harassment. It is probable, therefore, that the new offences of harassment will form the subject of many more criminal proceedings than the Government contemplates.

In his speech to the House of Lords on 24 January 1997, the Lord Chancellor stated that '. . . there is a great deal to be said for building on civil sanction-type provisions' (Hansard, 24 January 1997, col. 941). This suggests that the Government's intention is for the offence to be 'civil led', i.e., victims will initially be expected to obtain civil injunctions under s. 3 of the Act. The police and the Crown Prosecution Service would commence criminal proceedings only if that injunction was breached under s. 3(6).

The enforcement of civil injunctions by criminal proceedings may give rise to jurisprudential difficulties if only in relation to the burden of proof. The civil burden of proof is on a 'balance of probability' (more likely than not) and the criminal burden is 'beyond all reasonable doubt'. A person can presently be subjected to a civil injunction on a relatively low evidential test 'in the interests of justice'. He or she may not have committed any unlawful act. Yet breaching that injunction would be a criminal offence, even though otherwise no offence has been committed.

This issue was raised by Mr Andrew Bennett MP in debate in the House of Commons on 17 December 1996. His remarks are pertinent and are quoted from Hansard, 17 December 1996, col. 847, as follows:

I turn to the construction of clause 3, which begins with a civil remedy and builds a criminal offence on to that civil remedy. It is fairly unusual in this country for legislation to muddle criminal and civil court procedures, and we think that there are good reasons for keeping the two separate. The civil courts must balance the differing and conflicting interests of the two parties to the case. They have to decide between the two parties on the question of fairness. That is often extremely difficult, because the difference between the measure of proof on one side and the other may be fairly slim. The alternative approach of the criminal courts is that someone must be found guilty beyond all reasonable doubt.

I am worried about the fact that the issue will first be dealt with by civil proceedings, and if someone is in breach of those proceedings, instead of ensuring that the matter is taken up by the court as a contempt of court, we are creating a criminal offence. If we make a breach of an action in a civil court a criminal offence, we must make it clear that the same tests should be applied to the civil proceedings as would be applied in the criminal court. The standard of proof in the civil court should not be weaker than that applied in the criminal court.

If, as he suggests, the civil and criminal burdens of proof should be the same in relation to harassment, many of the principles in *Burris* v *Azadani* might not be applied by civil courts considering a statutory tort under the new Act. This could lead to a narrowing of the grounds, both factual and evidential, upon which civil courts will grant relief for harassment. It seems unfortunate that the Government should have muddied the waters in this way by mingling the civil and criminal law. The civil contempt procedure under the Act is further complicated by the absence of a power of arrest to minor domestic violence jurisdictions. What is proposed is that instead plaintiffs should make an *ex parte* application to the court for a warrant of arrest to be issued against the defendant.

Both authors — looking at s. 3(6) from their respective civil and criminal experience — consider that the provisions of s. 3 will be impractical, and civil practitioners may be well advised to deal with civil harassment cases in accordance with the normal civil procedures.

1.8   Progress of the Bill

The Bill passed swiftly through the Houses of Parliament. It was first published on 6 December 1996, and it completed its second reading and the committee stages in the House of Commons in two days on 17 and 18 December 1996. It had its second reading in the House of Lords on 24 January 1997. Although technically the third reading took place on 19 March 1997, it was never formally reconsidered by the House of Commons because of the calling of the general election. The Act received Royal Assent on 21 March 1997. Under s. 15 it will be brought into force by statutory instruments published either by the Home Secretary or by the Lord Chancellor. A timetable of the progress of the Bill is set out below:

Timetable: Protection from Harassment Act 1997

6 December 1996	Publication of Bill
	First reading in the House of Commons
17 December 1996	Second reading in the House of Commons
	Committee stage in Commons
18 December 1996	Completed committee stage in House of Commons
19 March 1997	Third reading in the House of Commons
21 March 1997	Royal Assent

Chapter 2
Criminal Harassment

2.1   Requirements of the offence

When the Protection from Harassment Bill was introduced into Parliament its overt purpose was simply to deal with the highly publicised problem of stalking. The Act, however, is worded so as to cover a far wider range of behaviour. The offence of criminal harassment created by s. 2 of the Act has the potential to become a widely used charge covering a large number of situations involving public disorder, conflict and dispute. Deciding what is and is not acceptable behaviour and whether particular incidents are trivial or significant lies at the heart of day-to-day policing and is also the essence of this Act. When it introduced the Act the Government estimated that there would be only 200 extra prosecutions per year brought because of it. That could well be a gross underestimate.

The offence of criminal harassment is created by a combination of ss. 1 and 2:

1.   Prohibition of harassment
  (1)   A person must not pursue a course of conduct—
    (a)   which amounts to harassment of another, and
    (b)   which he knows or ought to know amounts to harassment of the other.

2.   Offence of harassment
  (1)   A person who pursues a course of conduct in breach of section 1 is guilty of an offence.

Under s. 7(4) 'conduct' includes speech.

Criminal harassment is a summary only offence triable in the magistrates' court and carrying a possible sentence of up to six months' imprisonment and/or a fine not exceeding level 5 on the standard scale (£5,000). Under s. 2(3), police officers are given the power to arrest without warrant anyone reasonably suspected of having committed the offence. In addition, following conviction a magistrates' court can make a restraining order, breach of which carries a potential sentence of five years' imprisonment. Restraining orders are considered in more detail in chapter 5, but the possibility of a restraining order being made following conviction for the offence of criminal harassment gives this offence a significant potential. Low level, but repetitious, socially unacceptable behaviour could come to be dealt with by the courts far more severely than was possible before the Act. Whether that is desirable or not, only time will tell.

2.2   Relevance of civil cases

Because the definition in s. 1 applies to both the offence of criminal harassment and the civil tort, cases involving the Act in the civil courts will be as relevant as cases in the criminal courts in defining the offence of criminal harassment. While the legal distinction between the civil and criminal law will of course continue, in general any decisions of the Court of Appeal (Civil Division) regarding the tort of harassment created by s. 3 of the Act will be binding on any criminal courts considering the offence of criminal harassment.

2.3   Elements of the offence

To obtain a conviction for criminal harassment the prosecution will need to prove beyond reasonable doubt the three specific elements of harassment laid out in s. 1(1). The accused must pursue a course of conduct, the course of conduct must amount to harassment of another person, and the accused must know or ought to know that the course of conduct amounts to harassment.

2.4   Course of conduct

Course of conduct is defined in s. 7(3) as meaning 'conduct on at least two occasions', which makes criminal harassment an unusual charge. Normally criminal cases — particularly in the magistrates' courts — deal with one incident, but for the offence of criminal harassment to be proved the court will have to be satisfied that the conduct occurred on at least two occasions. Even though the course of conduct must involve two incidents there is no requirement that the incidents have to be the same each time. For example, a threat to steal property on a Monday followed by the breaking of a window on the Wednesday could constitute a course of conduct even though the conduct is different on each occasion.

2.5   Other offences

Appendix 4 details a number of existing criminal offences involving behaviour which is harassing in one way or another, but most criminal offences by their very nature cause harassment, alarm or distress to the victim of the crime. Since the offence of criminal harassment will involve conduct on at least two occasions, problems will arise where the conduct complained of constitutes an identifiable criminal offence on each occasion. For example, if A shouts obscenities at B one evening he commits an offence contrary to s. 5 of the Public Order Act 1986. If the behaviour is repeated the next evening then A has committed two offences contrary to s. 5 of the Public Order Act and has also pursued a course of conduct contrary to s. 2 of the Protection from Harassment Act. Theoretically, therefore, A could be charged with the two offences contrary to the Public Order Act, or with one offence of criminal harassment or with all three offences. There is no guidance in the Act as to which approach will be acceptable or preferred.

The problem is not completely unique, however. A burglar who goes to a house with burglary tools, breaks a window and burgles the house commits the separate offences of going equipped, criminal damage and burglary, but in practice will be charged only with the one offence of burglary which is considered to subsume the other offences. The same logic is likely to apply in cases of criminal harassment, and therefore it is unlikely that the courts will permit offenders to be tried for both criminal harassment and the separate offences which constitute the alleged course of conduct.

2.6   Choice between harassment and other charges

Where police have charged both criminal harassment and individual offences it is likely that the prosecution will be required to elect whether they wish to deal with individual incidents by separate charges, or whether they wish to lump them together in one charge of criminal harassment. In many respects the one charge of criminal harassment would be the better choice because the victim will have to give evidence only once, and if the defendant is convicted the court will be able to make a restraining order preventing future offending. However, if the evidence is weak on one of the two alleged incidents then on a charge of criminal harassment the prosecution will face the danger that the defendant will have to be acquitted because only one of the two incidents can be proved. Prosecutors will need to make careful decisions as to which choice to make in these cases, while defence lawyers will have to be equally careful to ensure that the prosecution are obliged to make a choice and are not permitted to have 'two bites of the cherry' by proceeding on both criminal harassment and separate charges.

Another possibility that prosecutors may find attractive would be to charge the first incident as a substantive offence and to charge criminal harassment after the second incident with the intention of having the trial for the first incident held before the trial for criminal harassment. That would then allow them to prove the first incident in the criminal harassment trial by producing a certificate of conviction under ss. 73 and 74 of the Police and Criminal Evidence Act 1984, and they would only have to call evidence to establish the facts of the second incident. Such an approach is likely to be regarded by the courts as an abuse of process, however. In *R* v *Forest of Dean Justices ex parte Farley* [1990] RTR 288, the defendant was charged with drink driving and with dangerous driving. The prosecution wished to deal with the trial for drink driving first, with the intention of then using the drink driving conviction as evidence in the dangerous driving trial. The Divisional Court decided that the tactic amounted to an abuse and the prosecution should proceed with the more serious trial first.

2.7 Relevance of previous convictions

More difficult problems would arise if a defendant has already been convicted of an earlier offence before the second incident occurs. It is far from clear whether the earlier conviction could be used as evidence in a criminal harassment trial. On behalf of the defendant it could be argued that since the defendant had already been dealt with for the earlier offence, allowing it to be used to prove criminal harassment would in effect mean the defendant being punished twice for the same act. The contrary argument is that to prohibit the evidence of the earlier offence would frustrate the intent of an Act which was specifically passed in order to deal with behaviour on more than one occasion. One possible solution to this problem would be to allow the prosecution to put forward evidence of the facts of the earlier incident without the court being told that the defendant has already been convicted in relation to that earlier incident. That would permit the prosecution to establish the necessary course of conduct, but would avoid the court being prejudiced by knowing that the defendant has a previous conviction.

If the defendant was cautioned rather than charged on the earlier occasion then the situation is even more complicated. A caution is a written admission of guilt, but unlike a conviction there is no statutory provision allowing a caution to be proved by production of a certificate. It is likely that in any such case the courts will not allow the prosecution to produce the caution as evidence of the first incident and will insist that both incidents be specifically proved.

2.8 Time between incidents

Merely because there have been two incidents involving the same defendant and the same victim, that does not of itself necessarily prove that there has been a course of conduct. The distance in time between the two incidents is relevant. If a window is broken on one night and another a few nights later that would undoubtedly be a course of conduct, but what if the second window is broken six months or a year later? Clearly the longer the length of time between incidents the smaller the chance that they will constitute a course of conduct; but it can be argued that even if the incidents are separated by a year they can still constitute a course of conduct. For example, an anti-semite who shouts obscenities outside a synagogue every Passover can clearly be said to be pursuing a course of conduct even though there is a period of a year between each incident.

At the other extreme, if there is only a short period of time between the two incidents they could be regarded as a course of conduct, or could be regarded as in reality just one incident. For example, an argument might occur between two neighbours where neighbour A shouts and swears at neighbour B, leaves and then five minutes later returns and starts shouting and swearing at B again. If this is regarded as one continuing incident then it merely constitutes an offence contrary to s. 5 of the Public Order Act 1986 and is punishable only with a fine. If, however, it is regarded as two incidents then it could constitute a course of conduct and so be punishable with up to six months' imprisonment. The difference is therefore significant, and defence lawyers in such a case would undoubtedly argue strongly that it should be regarded as one continuing incident.

In looking for guidance on whether particular actions constitute a course of conduct the courts may try to draw analogies with r. 9 of the Indictment Rules 1971. This deals with joinder of different charges in one indictment where the charges constitute 'part of a series of offences of the same or a similar character'. In *Ludlow* v *Metropolitan Police Commissioner* [1970] 2 WLR 521, the House of Lords decided that both the legal and factual characteristics of separate incidents were relevant in determining their similarity, and that for separate offences to be described as a series there had to be some nexus between them, i.e., 'some feature of similarity which in all the circumstances of the case enables the offences to be described as a series'. It is likely that courts will look for similar 'features of similarity' in deciding whether particular incidents constitute a course of conduct.

2.9   Harassment of another

Sections 1 and 2 collectively make it an offence to pursue a course of conduct which amounts to harassment of another. Under s. 7(2) 'References to harassing a person include alarming the person or causing the person distress'. Harassment, alarm and distress are not defined in the Act and so will need to be given their ordinary dictionary meanings, but they are words used in ss. 4A and 5 of the Public Order Act 1986 and therefore cases involving those provisions will be relevant in interpreting the 1997 Act.

Sections 4A and 5 of the Public Order Act 1986 require harassment, alarm or distress to be caused by the use of threatening, abusive or insulting words or behaviour, or disorderly behaviour, or by the display of any writing, sign or other visible representation which is threatening, abusive or insulting. Under the 1997 Act there is no such requirement. This arises because of the fact that the initial impetus behind the Act was to deal with stalkers who invariably had no intention of threatening, abusing or insulting those they were stalking. Someone who stands every day outside a house with a notice saying 'I love you', or who sends red roses to a person's place of work every day is certainly not being threatening, abusive or insulting, but could still be causing harassment, alarm or distress.

2.10   Defining harassment

In dealing with cases under ss. 4A and 5 of the Public Order Act 1986, the courts have been reluctant to define with any precision precisely what behaviour can or cannot constitute harassment. In *Lodge* v *Director of Public Prosecutions* (1988) *The Times*, 26 October, the Divisional Court held that whether someone, in that case a police officer, had been caused harassment, alarm or distress was a question of fact to be determined by the magistrates, and unless the magistrates' decision was totally perverse the High Court would not interfere. The lack of any precise definition or examples in the Act, combined with this *laissez-faire* attitude on the part of the High Court, means that the offence of criminal harassment is potentially extremely wide-ranging with regard to the situations in which it will apply.

Parking a car every day outside a neighbour's driveway as he is about to go to work could be harassment, as could starting up a lawnmower every time neighbours go out to sunbathe. In Northern Ireland, an Orange band playing 'The Protestant Boys' outside a Catholic church every Sunday could constitute harassment, as could standing with an Israeli flag outside a mosque.

In *Director of Public Prosecutions* v *Orum* [1988] 3 All ER 449, the Divisional Court held that it was possible, though unlikely, that individual police officers could be harassed, alarmed or distressed by words used toward them, though (as the court stated) in most cases 'words and behaviour with which police officers will be wearily familiar will have little emotional impact on them save boredom'.

Almost any form of activity which annoys another person could technically be defined as harassment. Shouting 'hello fatty' every time your neighbour comes in sight or 'here comes useless' every time a fellow employee enters the office are obvious examples, but there are many possible acts which could have the effect of causing harassment. Sexual harassment, for example, could include commenting on the length of a colleague's skirt, or putting 'pinups' on a notice board. Racial harassment could be caused not just by overt racial insults but by having cartoons on the wall dealing with missionaries in cannibal pots. Often it is not the overt act itself which is harassing but the known, but unprovable, motives of the person involved. Complaints are likely to be met by the argument that the person complaining 'cannot take a joke'.

It is of course true that certain people are unusually sensitive and have a tendency to overreact to the normal irritations of day-to-day life. There is a danger, therefore, that the criminal courts could find themselves being asked to adjudicate on neighbour disputes where in reality one or both parties simply need to grow up.

2.11   Alarm and distress

The fact that under s. 7(2) harassment includes alarm and distress should not be overlooked. There are situations where persons could be alarmed or distressed without themselves being the direct target of the course of conduct.

In *Lodge* v *Director of Public Prosecutions* (1988) *The Times*, 26 October, for example, the Divisional Court held that a police officer could feel alarm over the safety of another person, in that case a child. The same principle must logically apply to the Act. For example, a man might be in the habit of regularly hanging around near a school giving sweets to the children or following them home. He might not be harassing the children, and even if he was nobody would want to call them as witnesses in a court. However, his behaviour might cause alarm to the headmaster of the school, or to certain parents or the local community police officer. If he is asked to stop what he is doing and he continues then he has engaged in a course of conduct which has caused alarm and he can be charged with criminal harassment.

If an animal rights protester distributed or displayed to the public particularly graphic and bloody pictures of animals killed in hunts or used in experiments then members of the public could be caused distress. If this distress was caused more than once then arguably the protester would be guilty of criminal harassment. It is likely that the courts will attempt to limit the scope of ss. 1 and 2 by insisting that the course of conduct must be directed towards a specified person or persons rather than being 'at large'. Such an interpretation would certainly be in line with the intentions of Parliament when the Act was passed.

2.12   Defences to a charge of criminal harassment

A specific purpose of the Act was to deal with what were perceived to be inadequacies in the existing law. The main problem was that almost all criminal offences required some evidence of intent on behalf of the alleged offender. The solution adopted in s. 1(2) of the Act was to consider harassment objectively in terms of what actually happened rather than subjectively in terms of what the offender intended.

1.   Prohibition of harassment

(2)   For the purposes of this section, the person whose course of conduct is in question ought to know that it amounts to harassment of another if a reasonable person in possession of the same information would think the course of conduct amounted to harassment of the other.

The idea of the 'reasonable man' (today the reasonable person) is an old one in English law, but what exactly will be considered reasonable is almost impossible to predict with any certainty. What is considered 'reasonable' can differ from place to place and person to person. For example, the behaviour of a football supporter who shouts obscenities at the referee during a premier league football match may be considered acceptable, but similar remarks would be completely unacceptable if they were shouted at the referee during a primary school football competition. A car with a loud stereo system may be ignored on the M6 but cause immense annoyance in a quiet country village. Everything will depend on the place, the time and the people involved.

Under s. 1(3) it is a defence to a charge of criminal harassment for the accused to show in relation to a course of conduct:

(a)   that it was pursued for the purpose of preventing or detecting crime,

(b)   that it was pursued under any enactment or rule of law or to comply with any condition or requirement imposed by any person under any enactment, or

(c)   that in the particular circumstances the pursuit of the course of conduct was reasonable.

It is noticeable that there is no defence of being engaged in a lawful occupation such as a journalist, a private detective or, incidentally, a lawyer cross-examining a witness. It is likely that the main persons who will be protected by this particular defence will be police officers and bailiffs who will be carrying out their lawful duties. Anyone else will have to prove that their actions were reasonable.

When the Government was undertaking its consultation process prior to the Bill being published, fears were expressed that certain officials, such as MI5 agents engaged in intelligence activities, could fall foul of any stalking law. For that reason s. 12 of the Act provides that where a Government minister certifies that any actions undertaken by a specified person related to:

    (a)   national security;
    (b)   the economic well-being of the United Kingdom; or
    (c)   the prevention or detection of serious crime;

and were done on behalf of the Crown then the certificate is conclusive evidence that the Act does not apply. In practice the Government is not likely to want to publicise any incident where a certificate might be appropriate. Any criminal charges in such a case are more likely to be quietly dropped by the Crown Prosecution Service, and in cases involving a private prosecution the prosecution is likely to be taken over by the CPS and then discontinued.

2.13 Stalkers

Despite the fact that stalking provided the impetus for the Act, there is no definition of 'stalking' contained within it. In the Private Member's Bill introduced in May 1996 by Janet Anderson MP, stalking was defined as:

… engaging in a course of conduct whereby a person
    (a)   follow, loiters near, watches or approaches another person
    (b)   telephones (which for the avoidance of doubt shall include telephoning a person but remaining silent during the call), contacts by other electronic means, or otherwise contacts another person
    (c)   loiters near, watches, approaches or enters a place where another person lives, works or repeatedly visits
    (d)   interferes with property which does not belong to him and is in the possession of another person
    (e)   leaves offensive, unwarranted or unsolicited material at a place where another person lives, works or regularly visits
    (f)   gives offensive, unwarranted or unsolicited material to another person.

Section 264 of the Canadian Criminal Code defines criminal harassment (stalking) as:

    (a)   repeatedly following from place to place the other person or anyone known to them

(b)   repeatedly communicating with, either directly or indirectly, the other person or anyone known to them

(c)   besetting or watching the dwelling house, or place where the other person, or anyone known to them, resides, works, carries on business or happens to be

(d)   engaging in threatening conduct directed at the other person or any member of their family.

It is almost certain that any of the above types of behaviour would be regarded as criminal harassment under the Act, and certainly it was that type of persistent stalking behaviour that Parliament had in mind when the Act was passed.

2.14   Effect on journalists

Journalists and press photographers could easily find themselves accused of criminal harassment since the nature of their work will often involve attempting to speak to or to take photographs of persons who do not desire their attentions. It is not uncommon for people in the news suddenly to find that their home is in effect under siege by massed ranks of reporters and cameramen. Such behaviour can quite often cause harassment, and even if the police and CPS decide not to press charges there is nothing in the Act to prevent private prosecutions.

It is difficult to predict just how the courts will react when journalists and photographers appear before them charged with criminal harassment, but it will certainly happen at some point. It is probable that in such cases the courts will adopt the legitimate interests test laid down by the Court of Appeal in the civil case of *Burris* v *Azadani* [1995] 4 All ER 802 and will attempt to balance the legitimate public interest in a free press with the right of individuals not to be harassed. An important element in making such a judgment may be whether the person allegedly being harassed has in some way brought the press interest on himself or herself. That has certainly been the approach adopted by the American courts in considering press freedom and the First Amendment to the United States Constitution. A Government minister who is discovered to be having an affair may therefore be fair game for massed photographers, but the relatives of someone who has been murdered will not. However, what if the person being investigated is a suspected, but not proved, fraudster? Investigative journalists such as Roger Cook often have to lie in wait for such people who have good reasons to be reluctant to be interviewed about their business activities. Robert Maxwell was notoriously quick to issue libel writs in order to prevent scrutiny of his activities, and it could well be that other, lesser, fraudsters would be equally quick to take out private prosecutions for harassment in order to prevent journalistic investigation of their activities.

2.15   Protesters

It is possible that the Act could be used to stifle lawful protests. Anti-blood sports activists regularly attend fox hunts and attempt to disrupt them by blocking roads, blowing horns etc. Hunters could claim that these actions cause them harassment, and in a rural area such hunters are likely to have the support of the local police and magistrates. If convicted of criminal harassment the anti-blood sports protesters could then be subjected to a restraining order banning them from going near another hunt. Any such attempt to use the Act in this way would arguably be in breach of Article 11 of the European Convention of Human Rights but is possible.

Anti-roads protests are becoming more frequent and usually involve protesters attempting to prevent workmen cutting down trees, using earth-moving equipment etc. This could be considered to be harassment of the workmen rendering the protesters liable to arrest and prosecution.

2.16 Noise harassment

Noise is increasingly being recognised as a social problem and offenders can be prosecuted under the Environmental Protection Act 1990; however, the procedures for prosecution are complex and slow. Noise is often a particular problem in neighbour disputes, with music turned up loud or playing late into the night. Large numbers of dogs, or dogs which howl or whine incessantly can cause immense mental distress to neighbours, as can people who are constantly engaged in noisy do-it-yourself house repairs, or car repairs involving revving of engines.

Noise pollution is technically a local authority matter rather than a police responsibility, but frequently the police become involved when the neighbour dispute gets out of hand. It is quite possible that the police will be tempted to lay charges of criminal harassment in such cases, or neighbourhood groups may commence private prosecutions.

2.17 Northern Ireland

When the Protection from Harassment Bill was first introduced into Parliament it did not cover Northern Ireland, but s. 13 was added to the Bill during the committee stage and allows the Act to be extended to Northern Ireland. This was obviously done on the basis that stalking should be criminalised throughout the entire United Kingdom. What does not seem to have been considered, however, was the possibility that the definition of harassment in the Act could have particular significance in relation to the sectarian divide in Ulster.

Over the last few years the subject of Orange Lodge marches through predominantly Catholic areas has become an increasingly bitter issue in Northern Ireland politics, with a potentially dangerous stand-off between marchers and police in the town of Drumcree. It could be argued that marchers going annually through an area where they are not welcome are engaged in a course of conduct which they know or ought to know is causing harassment, alarm or distress to the inhabitants of that area. In those circumstances the police, or private individuals, could bring charges of criminal harassment against several of the principal marchers and attempt to obtain restraining orders preventing them from marching through the neighbourhood again.

It is doubtful whether any such approach would do anything to help the situation in Northern Ireland, but it is a possibility which cannot be ignored.

2.18   Plea bargaining

As is discussed in more detail in chapter 5, the fact that conviction under s. 2 will allow courts to make a restraining order will inevitably lead to plea bargaining. Where defendants are charged under s. 2, defence lawyers may well offer pleas to alternative offences (see Appendix 4) in order to avoid a restraining order being made. Where defendants are charged with other more serious offences, defence lawyers may offer to plead to a charge under s. 2 on the basis that they would agree to a restraining order being made. In cases involving vulnerable or nervous witnesses, such an offer may well be attractive to both prosecutors and courts.

Chapter Three
The Statutory Tort of Harassment

3.1 Introduction

Hitherto, the civil law of harassment has been greatly misunderstood by practitioners. There appears to be a great gulf between the apparent willingness of the courts to grant relief in harassment cases on the one hand and the apparent reluctance of practitioners to marshall cases and to apply for such relief on the other hand. This gulf is undoubtedly caused by a misunderstanding of the way in which the courts approach the issue of harassment. The purpose of this chapter is to seek to dispel the myths that surround this area of law and to alert practitioners to the essential principles with which the courts are concerned.

Some of these principles are as follows and particularly apply to the considerations applied to injunctive relief:

(a) The courts will interfere in all cases where the behaviour of an alleged harasser requires the intervention of the court, whatever that behaviour may be.

(b) The courts' jurisdiction will not necessarily be fettered by whether or not a cause of action exists in strict law, or whether or not the behaviour is or is not lawful or unlawful in the strict sense. A broad approach will be adopted and causes of action construed accordingly.

(c) The courts are prepared to offer injunctive relief to prohibit behaviour which would otherwise be regarded as lawful. Thus concentrating on proving the unlawfulness of the defendant's behaviour is not necessarily the dominant consideration.

(d) The primary consideration is whether or not the legitimate interests of the alleged victim are adversely affected sufficiently to justify curtailing or injuncting the behaviour of the alleged harasser.

(e) Thus the courts are concerned with the principle of legitimate interests, which may be widely defined and may not necessarily encompass interests which are formally regarded as capable of protection in strict law.

(f) In determining whether to injunct an alleged harasser the courts will consider the legitimate interests of the respective parties and will balance their respective interests. Thus an imbalance which seriously infringes the legitimate interests of one party may be rectified by injunctive relief.

The practitioner who wishes to approach the law of harassment by reference to strictly defined causes of action, and lawful or proscribed behaviour, will be disappointed. What is clear is that the courts wish to adopt a flexible, pragmatic and commonsense approach to this whole area of what can be regarded as conflict in society. Any behaviour which is 'more than anti-social behaviour', or behaviour which is 'of concern' is sufficient to invoke an investigation by the court under s. 3 of the Act. The starting point will be whether the behaviour has a serious impact on the victim's freedom and adversely affects his or her quality of life. A relatively low burden of proof is placed on the plaintiff seeking an interlocutory injunction. This is clearly stated in the *dicta* of the Master of the Rolls in *Burris* v *Azadani* [1995] 4 All ER 802, p. 807 at D:

> It is of course quite clear that the court cannot properly grant an injunction unless the plaintiff can show at least an arguable cause of action to support the grant, but subject to this overriding requirement section 37 [Supreme Court Act 1981], as has often been observed, is cast in the widest terms.

This development is paralleled by the criminal law which is convicting defendants of assault who have neither committed battery on their victims nor have they, in the strictest sense, caused them to experience an immediate fear of violence. Thus the traditional principles of assault appear to have been radically developed by the Court of Appeal in *Burstow* (psychological assault) and *Ireland* (telephone assault) (see 1.3 above).

Section 3(1) creates a statutory tort of harassment:

3.   Civil remedy

(1)   An actual or apprehended breach of section 1 may be the subject of a claim in civil proceedings by the person who is or may be the victim of the course of conduct in question.

Subject to the definition of intention and the defences provided by s. 1(3), the ingredients of the tort are as follows:

(a)   either an actual course of conduct which amounts to harassment of another; or

(b)   an apprehended course of conduct which would (if perpetrated) amount to harassment of another; and

(c)   a person who is (under (a) above) or may be (under (b) above) the victim of such a course of conduct.

Thus the essential elements of this statutory tort are:

(a)   a course of conduct, actual or apprehended; *understood*

(b)   harassment of another, whether actual or apprehended; *understanding of*

(c)   a victim, whether actual or prospective. *expected*

The only statutory definition of these ingredients is contained in s. 7 and is as follows:

7.   Interpretation of this group of sections

(2)   References to harassing a person include alarming the person or causing the person distress.

(3)   A 'course of conduct' must involve conduct on at least two occasions.

(4)   'Conduct' includes speech.

The essential areas for consideration are:

(a)   a definition of what the courts consider or are likely to consider amounts to harassment, whether actual or apprehended;

(b)   the manner in which the civil courts are likely to deal with allegations of harassment;

(c)   who is or may be a victim of harassment;

(d)   the definition of alarming or causing distress.

3.2   The definition of harassment

When discussing the vagueness of the definition of the analogous tort of personal injury by molestation, Brazier, 'Personal Injury by Molestation — an Emergent or Established Tort' [1992] FLR 346 states:

> ... flexibility enables the court to make a commonsense judgment based on a determination of when intrinsic and unpleasant conduct exceeds the bounds of what society will tolerate and poses a risk of damage to an individual's fundamental right to freedom from injury.

The 1997 Act clearly contemplates a commonsense judgment as to what 'a reasonable person in possession of the same information [as the defendant] would think ... amounted to harassment' (s. 1(2)).

Unlike the tort of personal injury by molestation (where it must be proven that the defendant intended to and did cause personal injury), the wording in s. 3(1) of the Act defines the victim not by reference to actual suffering as a result of harassment, but by reference to the course of conduct in question.

Matters are compounded by the words 'apprehended breach' and 'person who ... may be the victim'. This wording clearly provides for a cause of action in respect of perceived harassment which has not yet occurred, and indeed may never occur. This section can prohibit possible or potential behaviour and is very wide. Strong evidence would be needed to persuade a court to prohibit a course of behaviour which has not yet manifested itself.

From the debates recorded in Hansard it is clear that the intention of Parliament is not to seek to define various categories of behaviour which might amount to harassment. When considering whether harassment should be defined by reference to a list of prohibited activities, David MacLean, Home Office Junior Minister, discussed the problem of stalking in the Commons debate (Hansard, 17 December 1996, col. 827). His remarks apply to any form of harassing behaviour, however, not just stalking:

> Stalkers do not stick to the activities on a list. Stalkers and other weirdos who pursue women, cause racial harassment and annoy their neighbours have a wide range of activity which it is impossible to define.

In the debate in the House of Lords on 24 January 1997, the Lord Chancellor offered helpful remarks on the definition of harassment as follows:

> No one who has looked at the problem with any degree of concentration could possibly think that it is easy to define the basic elements of ... [harassment]. I am grateful to the Noble Earl, Lord Russell, for the advice that he was given by a student. I believe that he found it even more valuable than the multitude of legal advice to which he had access. It was a useful analysis of the concept. He said first, it is driving me round the bend. That is harassment. It is a continuation of the matter. Secondly it was unwelcome: that is an important criterion. He said that the activity went on and on. That makes for a course of conduct. He also said 'I did not want it'. Those are the elements of harassment. There is a lot to be said for that analysis, but the same conditions might apply to an investigative journalist seeking to interview some magnate who is accused of a corrupt practice.

It is clear, therefore, that the definition of what amounts to harassment is meant to be construed by reference to the ordinary standards of reasonable persons in society. This definition is clearly going to give rise to a great deal of argument as to what is understood by the word 'reasonable', because it is construed in different ways by different persons in different circumstances. What is regarded as reasonable behaviour in Belgravia may not necessarily be regarded as reasonable behaviour in Barrow-in-Furness. Any behaviour will need to be serious enough to cause the courts to be concerned for the person who is the recipient, whether actual or apprehended. Such behaviour will need to constitute an enforced form of involuntary contact imposed upon the victim which cannot be justified and which the victim is entitled to be freed from.

3.3. The manner in which the civil courts may consider allegations of harassment

(a) Previous judicial approaches
The meaning of 'molestation' under the Domestic Violence and Matrimonial Proceedings Act 1976 was discussed by Ormrod LJ in *Horner* v *Horner* [1982] 2 All

ER 495 at p. 497, who commented that 'for my part I have no doubt that molesting in section 1(1)(a) of the 1976 Act does not imply necessarily either violence or threats of violence. It applies to any conduct which can properly be regarded as such a degree of harassment as to call for the intervention of the court'. Thus, when considering a course of alleged molestation at common law, the court is engaged in evaluating the degree to which the defendant's behaviour exceeds the bounds of ordinary behaviour and assessing whether the conduct of the defendant was likely to cause harm to the victim.

As was stated by Lord Bridge in *McLoughlin v O'Brian* [1982] 2 All ER 298, the law expects the ordinary person to bear certain mishaps of life with 'customary phlegm', but the law does not expect ordinary young women to bear indefinitely a campaign of harassment as in that case. It is submitted that, when considering the civil remedy under s. 3(1) of the Act, the courts will be more concerned with the campaign or course of harassing behaviour than with the damage which may or may not be inflicted as a result. Often, of course, it is impossible to separate the two. However, any course of conduct which interferes with the 'legitimate interests' (see below) of a victim are prima facie actionable under s. 3(1).

(b)   The principle of the legitimate interests of the victim

This principle is clearly set out in the Court of Appeal decision of *Burris v Azadani* [1995] 4 All ER 802, which arguably created the civil (common law) tort of harassment for the first time. Previously, it had been argued, any tort of harassment was subsumed within the torts of nuisance, trespass or interference with the person. The judgment in *Burris v Azadani* is extremely important and needs to be considered very carefully by all those concerned with the law of harassment.

Throughout his judgment, Sir Thomas Bingham MR repeatedly used the words 'legitimate interests', even apparently distinguishing such interests from those which are capable of being protected in tort. In doing so, he made it clear that the civil courts will adopt a commonsense approach to the subject of harassment, and will not necessarily seek to limit relief depending upon whether or not the facts fall within a principle of established tort law.

Sir Thomas Bingham MR compared the exclusion zone order in *Burris v Azadani* (see below) to the exercise by the High Court of its *Mareva* jurisdiction:

> A *Mareva* injunction granted in the familiar form restrains a defendant from acting in a way which is not, in itself, tortious or otherwise unlawful. . . . The court recognises a need to protect the legitimate interests of those who have invoked its jurisdiction . . . it would not seem to me to be a valid objection to the making of an exclusion zone order that the conduct to be restrained is not in itself tortious or otherwise unlawful if such an order is reasonably regarded as necessary for the protection of a plaintiff's legitimate interests. ([1995] 4 All ER 802, at p. 807)

Thus, legitimate interests are those which the court will protect in their own right. It is clear that the common law will restrain behaviour which would otherwise be regarded as lawful behaviour in order to protect such interests. This is a vital distinction between the criminal and the civil law. The purpose of criminal law is to punish defendants for acting unlawfully. The primary purpose of the civil law, in this area, is to restrain defendants, who may otherwise apparently be acting lawfully, from infringing legitimate interests of a plaintiff which are wrongly infringed by such apparently lawful behaviour. This is a formula which the criminal courts cannot adopt, because criminal defendants can be convicted only once unlawful behaviour has been proven. Of course it is a criminal offence to breach a civil injunction granted under s. 3(3) of the Act, and this represents a new departure of the law.

Much of the relief afforded by the court to protect legitimate interests will be limited to injunctive relief: 'Ordinarily the victim will be adequately protected by an injunction which restrains the tort which has been or is likely to be committed, whether trespass to the person or land, interference with goods, harassment, intimidation or as the case may be.' ([1995] 4 All ER 802, at p. 811)

It is clear that the courts are prepared to protect legitimate interests when such interests are threatened by behaviour which is otherwise lawful. This is demonstrated by the decision of Scott J in *Thomas v National Union of Mineworkers* [1986] Ch 20. He held that working miners were entitled to use the public highway to enter their place of work without unreasonable harassment. His judgment reiterates the adoption of a commonsense approach to this area, and one which is not concerned with limiting relief to established principles of law: 'The tort might be described as a species of private nuisance, namely unreasonable interference with victims' rights to use the highway. But the label for the tort does not, in my view, matter.'

(c)   The balance of interests test

An understanding of the way in which the civil courts balance the respective interests of the relevant parties is fundamental to an understanding of the manner in which they are likely to view the statutory tort of harassment. Civil courts are almost exclusively concerned with private law and with relative behaviour. Criminal courts are primarily concerned with public law and with absolute notions of behaviour, with defendants being convicted if they act contrary to prohibited precepts of criminal law. Thus when considering the legitimate interests of the plaintiff the civil court will balance such interests against the legitimate interests of the defendant. This test, and the way it works, is described in the *dicta* of the (then) Master of the Rolls in *Burris v Azadani* (at pp. 810–11) as follows:

There are two interests to be reconciled. One is that of the defendant. His liberty must be respected up to the point at which his conduct infringes, or threatens to infringe, the rights of the plaintiff. No restraint should be placed on him which is not judged to be necessary to protect the rights of the plaintiff. But the plaintiff has an interest which the court must be astute to protect. The rule of law requires that those whose rights are infringed should seek the aid of the court, and respect for the legal process can only suffer if those who need protection fail to get it ... respect for the freedom of the aggressor should never lead the court to deny necessary protection to the victim. ...

This test is put thus by Schiemann LJ (at pp. 811–12):

> There are in these cases two interests to be reconciled — that of the plaintiff not to be harassed and that of the defendant to be allowed to move freely along the highway. An exclusion zone interferes with the latter in order to secure the former. On its face it forbids what are lawful actions. The defendant has rendered himself liable to such an order because of his previous harassing behaviour. Nonetheless the judge imposing such an order must be careful not to interfere with the defendant's right more than is necessary in order to protect the plaintiff.

Thus any order made by the civil court, which will ordinarily be injunctive, will seek to protect the plaintiff's 'legitimate interests' against acts of a defendant which may not necessarily be tortious. The order will be tailored so that it limits the manner in which it infringes the defendant's liberty only to what is strictly necessary in order to protect the interests of the plaintiff.

3.4 The definition of victims of harassment

It has already been submitted (see 3.3) that s. 3(1) defines the victim not by reference to actual suffering as a result of harassment, but by reference to the course of conduct in question. Thus a victim, for the purposes of obtaining injunctive relief under s .3(1), must establish that he or she is the subject or may be the subject of a course of harassment and that his or her legitimate interests are being or may be interfered with. No actual loss need be proven in order to obtain injunctive relief. All that need be proven is the unreasonable, and by definition wrongful, infringement (actual or threatened) of the legitimate interests of the victim after a consideration of the balance of interests test. In criminal law it is clear that intention to harass must be proven on the objective test, i.e., would a reasonable person think that the course of conduct amounted to harassment. In civil law it is submitted that the question of intention arises only as a subsidiary rather than a dominant issue. The issue is not necessarily the intention of the defendant but rather the need to protect the legitimate interests of the plaintiff.

What emerged in *Burris* v *Azadani* [1995] 4 All ER 802 was the principle of civil law that the need to protect a victim from aggression is paramount: '. . . respect for the freedom of the aggressor should never lead the court to deny necessary protection to the victim' (at p. 811). This principle does not rest easily in criminal law where the respect for the freedom of the aggressor is paramount up to the point where a breach of a fundamental precept of criminal law is perpetrated. Under the principle of legitimate interests, the Master of the Rolls defined these as 'the right of the victim to the courts' protection in relation to any behaviour which may be highly stressful and disturbing to a plaintiff'. This represents a departure from previous authorities which held that intimidatory behaviour was wrongful in tort only when accompanied by 'aggravating circumstances'. Thus previously the harasser who deliberately set out to inflict emotional harm, but stopped short of overt breaches of established law, was not normally answerable in common law unless his or her behaviour was extreme.

The limits of the previous law were set out by the authority of *Wilkinson* v *Downton* [1897] 2 QB 57. The facts of this case were that the defendant, as a joke, told Mrs Wilkinson that her husband had been involved in an accident in which he had broken both his legs. As a result of receiving this false information, the plaintiff suffered a 'violent shock to her nervous system producing vomiting and other serious and permanent physical consequences at one time threatening her reason'. Clearly the plaintiff had suffered harm (in the form of nervous shock) as a consequence of the deliberate behaviour of the defendant, but such harm did not flow directly for the purposes of the tort of trespass. However, the principle of law expressed by Wright J gave the plaintiff a cause of action where 'the defendant has ... wilfully done an act calculated to cause physical harm to the plaintiff, that is to say to infringe a legal right to personal safety and has in fact thereby caused physical harm to her. The proposition without more appears to state a good cause of action'.

Wilkinson v *Downton* is remarkable because it unproblematically classified intentionally inflicted nervous shock as physical harm and as actionable at a time when a cause of action did not exist in the context of negligence. Also it founded a cause of action for remedying the general wrong of wilfully engaging in an act 'calculated to cause physical harm'. Thus this case, which is one hundred years old, is authority for the proposition that the courts will be flexible in founding causes of action in granting relief in cases of harassment. The principal difference between *Wilkinson* v *Downton* and the civil remedy proposed by s. 3(1) is that under the former the plaintiff is still required to prove actual physical harm in the form of impairment to health; under the latter all that need be proved is a course or intended course of harassment.

This principle has been developed by the parallel tort of personal injury by molestation. The judgment in *Burnett* v *George* [1992] 1 FLR 525 recognised a broad category of conduct which had infringed the plaintiff's right to personal safety where the defendant's conduct was calculated to cause harm to the plaintiff. In that case the Court of Appeal accepted that molestation which causes injury to mental or physical health may amount to a tort. The Court granted an injunction to restrain harassment by telephone calls. The plaintiff complained of 'a series of molestation and assaults ... assaults upon her person ... harassment by means of telephone calls at unsocial hours'. The court of first instance had restrained the defendant from conduct amounting to molestation and interference with the plaintiff. However, the Court of Appeal held that the plaintiff's health had not been impaired by the course of conduct perpetrated by the defendant. Accordingly the Court of Appeal amended the injunction imposed by the trial judge to prohibit molestation and interference calculated to impair the plaintiff's health.

As *Burnett* v *George* is a fairly recent decision of the Court of Appeal, which is concerned with the analogous and parallel tort of personal injury by molestation, it cannot be ignored. However, it is submitted that under s. 3(1) it is not necessary to prove injury or impairment of the plaintiff's health. It is sufficient that there is a course of conduct which amounts to molestation or interference which can therefore be defined as harassment. Thus the Court of Appeal would not now limit any injunctive remedy to acts calculated to impair the plaintiff's health.

It is clear, therefore, that there has been a radical shift in the civil law away from focusing on any damage caused to the victim, to concentrating upon the actions of the alleged harasser. This contrasts with the criminal law which has shifted away from concentrating upon the actions of the defendant to a consideration of the effect of his or her behaviour on the alleged victim. It appears to be a paradox that the principles of civil and criminal law seem to have been reversed, at least in relation to the law of harassment. Thus a defendant, whether civil or criminal, who has engaged in anti-social conduct of a serious kind can find himself or herself the subject of a civil injunction or a criminal conviction even though in the strictest sense the plaintiff cannot prove damages in law or the prosecutor cannot establish a conventional *actus reus*. Thus, civil law considers the conduct and not necessarily the consequences. Criminal law concentrates on the consequences and not necessarily the conduct.

In the Canadian case of *Motherwell* v *Motherwell* (1976) 73 DLR (3a) 62, Clement J commented that, although the persistent ringing of the telephone was likely to affect the nervous system, injury to health was not an essential element of the plaintiff's cause of action. Thus no special damage was required to support an injunction prohibiting such telephone harassment.

The judgment of Dillon LJ in *Khorasandjian* v *Bush* [1993] 3 All ER 669, at p. 676, echoed that of Clement J above:

So far as the harassing telephone calls are concerned, however, the inconvenience and annoyance to the occupier caused by such calls, and the interference thereby with the ordinary and reasonable use of the property are sufficient damage. The harassment is the persistent making of unwanted telephone calls, even apart from their content; if the content is itself, as here, threatening and objectionable, the harassment is the greater.

In applying the *Motherwell* v *Motherwell* decision, Dillon LJ and Roe LJ held that despite the fact that the plaintiff had no proprietary interest in the spouse's home, she was nonetheless entitled to a *quia timet* injunction to restrain a private nuisance in the form of persistent, unwanted telephone calls. The decision went a step further than *Motherwell* v *Motherwell*, since *Khorasandjian* v *Bush* involved a claim by a child of the family rather than a spouse, neither of whom had a strict proprietary interest in the cause of action of private nuisance. The decision in that case heralded the development of the tort of harassment in *Burris* v *Azadani* [1995] 4 All ER 802.

The dissenting judgment in *Khorasandjian* v *Bush* was given by Peter Gibson J, who insisted that the decision should have been founded under the tort of personal injury by molestation. He argued that the defendant should be prohibited from pestering or harassing only 'by doing acts calculated to cause the plaintiff harm'. However, Dillon LJ felt that the words were unnecessary because the Court was entitled to consider that the defendant's behaviour was plainly calculated to cause the plaintiff harm. The Court was entitled to find that the causation of harm to the plaintiff was the natural and probable consequence of the course of conduct which the defendant pursued, and from this it could be inferred that the defendant's acts were calculated to cause such harm to the plaintiff.

It is clear, therefore, that the courts will take judicial notice of the generally accepted principle that anyone who is harassed, depending on timescale and degree, will suffer impairment of health. Thus the focus of the courts is clearly on the course of conduct and whether it constitutes harassment. The prevailing judicial attitude encourages the provision of a solution on the basis that the rights of the victim are paramount.

3.5   The definition of alarming or causing distress

It has already been stated that the victim is defined not by the degree of injury suffered, but by reference to the course of harassing behaviour. Thus the court will concentrate not on the effect or potential effect on the victim, but on whether the course of conduct amounts to harassment. In determining the issue of harassment, the courts will consider the respective interests of the parties, and will balance such interests against each other to determine whether there has been harassment and (if so) whether it is actionable in law. It is clear that some forms of harassment are justified, depending on their degree, the timescale and the justification of the 'harasser'. Examples include a journalist 'robustly' pursuing a story, a debt collector seeking to induce payment of a debt or an ex-lover seeking to recover his or her chattels.

Under s. 7(2) 'harassing a person' includes causing alarm or distress. The courts will take judicial notice of the principle that, for example, constantly telephoning people during anti-social hours and breaking their sleep patterns will injure their health over a reasonably short period of time. In this respect, therefore, the test for causing alarm and distress is objective. However, the area of harassment is notoriously the province of the socially inadequate and the psychologically disturbed. Should a socially inadequate harasser who constantly seeks to communicate by writing or delivering roses (against the 'victim's' wishes) be liable in civil law for harassment? His state of mind might preclude him from the definition of a person who 'knows or ought to know' that the actions amount to harassment. A reasonable person might not consider that such conduct amounted to harassment.

Conversely, should an alleged harasser be responsible for the subjective effect that the course of conduct has on a person of low esteem, or on somebody who is psychologically impaired? He or she might not have known that the subject of his or her attentions suffered from low esteem and was therefore likely to be distressed or affected in a way which was totally unforeseeable to the perpetrator of the conduct in question.

These issues will doubtless need to be reviewed by the court. However, it is submitted that, as a general principle, established figures in our society — whether they be members of the Royal Family, politicians or media stars and celebrities —

should be deemed to have a higher 'distress' threshold than ordinary people who seek more privacy and more anonymity in their lives. However, it is clear that while a higher degree of distress is caused to those who are psychologically disturbed, nevertheless such persons are entitled to the protection of the courts if their 'legitimate interests' are being infringed. Clearly the right not to be harassed is more vital for someone who does not have the ordinary aptitude of the ordinary individual to combat such behaviour. It is of course arguable that if the harasser is aware of the victim's weakness, whether it be physical or psychological, then he or she ought to know that his or her behaviour would cause alarm or distress to that particular person. Thus the consideration of the respective legitimate interests of the parties and the application of the balance of interests test will be a necessary part of the consideration of this issue.

3.6   Defence to the civil tort of harassment

An absolute defence is laid down by s. 12(1):

12.   National security, etc.

(1)   If the Secretary of State certifies that in his opinion anything done by a specified person on a specified occasion related to —

   (a)   national security,

   (b)   the economic well-being of the United Kingdom, or

   (c)   the prevention or detection of serious crime,

and was done on behalf of the Crown, the certificate is conclusive evidence that this Act does not apply to any conduct of that person on that occasion.

Statutory defences are laid down by s. 1(3), which make it clear that a course of conduct is not defined as harassment if it is pursued for the purpose of preventing or detecting crime, under any rule of law (as widely defined in s. 1(3)(b)), or if 'in the particular circumstances the pursuit of the course of conduct was reasonable'.

So far as the civil practitioner is concerned, all these defences are summarised by the principles of 'legitimate interests' and the 'balance of interests' test between the plaintiff and the defendant. Whether or not a course of conduct is reasonable depends upon the respective legitimate interests of the relevant parties, and the balancing of those interests *inter se*. An illustration of the manner in which the courts will consider this is the case of *Diana Princess of Wales* v *Stenning* which did not proceed beyond the granting of an *ex parte* injunction on 15 August 1996. In that case the defendant purported to be a photographer. His principal activities concerned photographing Diana, Princess of Wales; and in order to do so he constantly shadowed her, in effect 'stalking her', even when she was engaged in strictly private activity. Responsible investigative journalists or photographers are clearly likely to show considerable interest in the actions of members of the Royal Family; and it is clear that the courts will be keen to protect the responsible activities of investigative journalists, in the general public interest that supports freedom of the press. However, the courts will balance the need for freedom of the press against the need to protect individuals from intrusive media interest (depending on all the circumstances). Any imbalance which is likely adversely to affect the alleged victim, or which cannot be justified under the principle of the legitimate interests of the press or otherwise, may be redressed under the statutory tort of harassment.

Consequently, the court will take into account all the relevant circumstances when considering whether a course of conduct is or remains reasonable, or whether it crosses the boundary and becomes unreasonable and anti-social. Adopting Ormrod LJ's definition in *Horner* v *Horner* (1983) 1 FLR 50, 'harassment' applies 'to any conduct which can properly be regarded as such a degree of harassment as to call for the intervention of the court'. It is clear, for instance, that the media interest displayed in Diana, Princess of Wales could, if directed at a more anonymous person and to the same scale, amount to harassment. It is a question of degree in each particular case. Some media stars can, depending on the circumstances, be regarded as 'fair game' for journalistic interests; but nevertheless, such interest cannot be infinite and must be subjected to limitation. Excess activity could amount to harassment.

3.7   Damages for the statutory tort of harassment

3.   Civil remedy

(2)   On such a claim, damages may be awarded for (among other things) any anxiety caused by the harassment and any financial loss resulting from the harassment.

As has been discussed above, it is likely that the relief which will be afforded by the courts in most cases involving harassment will be limited to injunctive relief. Nevertheless, tortfeasors are liable to pay damages to their victims, and s. 3(2) places the award of such damages on a statutory footing. Prima facie any harasser is liable to compensate the victim for any financial loss resulting from the course of conduct which amounts to harassment. However, the drafting of s. 3 suggests that the test for determining financial loss is causation and that damages are payable in respect of all financial loss resulting from the course of harassment.

This principle could have wide implications. Take, for instance, the harassing neighbour in a neighbourhood dispute. He makes life so intolerable for his victims that they decide to sell their house and move to another district. If the house is sold at a loss, is such loss a head of special damage and recoverable under this section? Furthermore, are the incidental costs and disbursements connected with the sale and purchase of another property also recoverable as special damages, whether they be estate agent's fees on the sale, conveyancing fees on the sale or purchase of an alternative property, stamp duty or land registry fees?

No doubt a great deal will depend upon the degree of harassment inflicted upon the victim, and whether it was reasonable for the victim to move house as a response to such a campaign of harassment. If the victim's response was reasonable, then it may be arguable that the financial loss resulting from the sale and purchase of a property was indeed the result of the course of harassment. Much will depend upon the facts of the particular case in question. The plaintiff's right to damages will be strengthened if the defendant received numerous warnings about his behaviour, the effect it was having upon the plaintiff, and the alternatives open to the plaintiff in the event that the course of harassment did not cease forthwith. This would call for the careful drafting of letters before action.

The same principles will apply to a victim who suffers from illness as a result of harassment and loses his or her job. Is the loss of earnings recoverable as special damages under s. 3?

Section 3(2) also provides for an award of damages in respect of anxiety caused by the harassment; and as the definition of harassing under s. 7(2) includes alarming the victim or causing the victim distress, it is submitted that damages will be awarded for anxiety, alarm or causing distress.

Mental distress takes many forms. The more outrageous and serious cases of harassment undoubtedly produce physical injury or nervous shock. Other forms of harassment cause fright, horror, grief, anger, embarrassment or humiliation.

For a long time the common law has been reluctant to award damages for distress because it has been concerned to restrict the range of actions where minor annoyances might be litigated. This is illustrated by Lord Wensleydale's generalisation in *Lynch* v *Knight* (1861) 9 HL Cas 577 that 'mental pain or anxiety, the law cannot value and does not pretend to redress, when the unlawful act complained of causes that alone'. The courts have, however, in a rather *ad hoc* manner, afforded legal redress for mental pain in the more serious cases, without formulating a wide general principle.

It is arguable that damages for anxiety also will be awarded only in more serious cases. Certainly this is the case in the USA. Section 46 of the American Law Institutes Second Restatement of Statutes (1966) provides as follows:

1. One who by extreme and outrageous conduct intentionally or recklessly causes severe emotional distress to another is subject to liability for such emotional distress.

Thus under that provision the conduct must be 'extreme and outrageous' and the emotional distress must be 'severe'.

The drafting of s. 3(2) provides that 'damages may be awarded for . . . any anxiety caused by the harassment'. Thus, prima facie, in relation to the statutory tort, *any* anxiety is sufficient to invoke the court's discretion to award damages, depending upon all the circumstances of the case. It must be considered, however, whether the anxiety so caused is to be tested objectively or subjectively. Clearly those of low social esteem, or those who suffer from a psychological disorder are much more susceptible to harassing behaviour than those of ordinary dispositions. Does the 'egg shell skull' principle apply to victims of anxiety, and does the harasser therefore have to take his victim as he finds him? Does the course of harassing behaviour have to be of a kind which is reasonably capable of causing mental distress to a normal human being, or is it sufficient that such distress was subjectively caused to that victim?

These are clearly matters which the courts will need to address. Nevertheless, it is equally clear that if the defendant knows of a particular susceptibility of the plaintiff, which is impaired or exaggerated as a result of the defendant's conduct, then the defendant cannot complain that mental distress would not have been caused to an ordinary person when it was clearly foreseeable that such distress would have been caused to that particular person by that particular conduct.

3.8 The practical application of section 3

The Act will clearly have a widespread impact on many areas of law, including those concerning the media, employment, neighbourhood disputes, protesters and the family. However, none of these areas is specifically addressed because the Act is concerned with the general question of protection from harassment. Practitioners dealing with specific problems within various specialisations will therefore need to understand the general principles which the civil courts will apply in harassment cases.

In essence the main principles are as follows:

(a)   Is there behaviour, or is there likely to be behaviour, which is sufficiently extreme to call for the intervention of the court?

(b)   Are the legitimate interests of the plaintiff being infringed, or are they likely to be infringed?

(c)   Does the defendant have a legitimate interest which entitles him or her to 'harass' the plaintiff?

(d)   How can the conflict be resolved once a balance of interests test between the parties has been conducted?

3.9 Domestic violence

The principles listed above are clearly mirrored in the domestic violence provisions of the Family Law Act 1996. It is not the intention of the authors to consider that Act in detail, but its purpose is to prevent violence, intimidation, harassment or pestering in the family home — known as 'cause for concern behaviour'. The 1996 Act is, however, limited to spouses, cohabitees, former spouses, former cohabitees and 'associated persons'. 'Associated persons' are defined in s. 62(3) and include relatives and persons who have agreed to marry. The definition does not include homosexual relationships, but it otherwise covers all those who have lived in the same household.

Persons who are not 'associated' within the definition of the Family Law Act 1996 will now have the opportunity to pursue claims for protection under the Protection from Harassment Act 1997. Such persons will include couples who associated together but who did not cohabit, work colleagues, neighbours etc.

3.10   Protesters

The principles listed at 3.8 may be re-stated as follows with regard to protesters:

(a)   Are the legitimate interests of the plaintiff being infringed, or are they likely to be infringed, by the protesters?

(b)   Do the protesters have a legitimate interest which entitles them to 'harass' the plaintiff?

(c)   How can the respective interests of the parties be reconciled using the balance of interests test?

Thus the main issue concerning protesters is not necessarily whether their behaviour amounts to harassment *per se* but whether their behaviour (which must amount to protesting) adversely affects the plaintiff's legitimate interests and cannot be justified by any legitimate interests which the protesters are entitled to exercise to the detriment of the plaintiff's legitimate interests.

The classic example of the legitimate protester is the striker. As a matter of public policy it has long been established that the legitimate interest of the striker (to withdraw labour) outweighs the legitimate interest of the employer (to enforce the contract of employment), although clearly the balance of interests test is applied to the general conduct of the parties in relation to other ancillary matters including peaceful picketing.

3.11   Hunt saboteurs

This is a topical subject and the application of the principles is as follows:

(a)   Are the hunt protesters infringing, or are they likely to infringe, the legitimate interests of the hunt?

(b)   Do the protesters have a legitimate interest which entitles them to infringe the plaintiffs' legitimate interests?

(c)   How can their interests be reconciled using the balance of interests test?

These principles were considered in the case of *Fitzwilliam Land Company* v *Cracknell* (unreported), September 1993. The court made it clear that it was not concerned with the morality of fox hunting or with the honestly held and deeply felt views on either side of the fox hunting lobby. Thus the general consideration of the legitimate interests of the parties is not necessarily to be governed by principles of morality (although such considerations could be relevant) but rather by principles of law.

Cracknell was a saboteur who persistently interfered with the hounds by hollering and by blowing a hunting horn. On numerous occasions this caused confusion to the hounds who were attracted away from the control of the huntsman. The hunt sued for trespass to goods, namely interference with the hounds. The court determined that the saboteur's conduct and the effect which it had on the hounds amounted to an actionable trespass even though consequential damages (in that particular case) could not be proved. (This of course limits the relief sought to injunctive relief.) Thus it was held that the protester clearly interfered with the plaintiff's legitimate interests, that he could not justify his conduct by a legitimate interest recognised in law (he could not argue that hunt protesting is socially acceptable in some circles and therefore fell within the term 'acceptable standard of conduct') and that the balance of interests test required the court to forbid the hunt protester 'from directly and deliberately interfering with the plaintiff's hounds by the use of noise whether by blowing a hunting horn, hollering or in any other manner'.

A hunt protester who trespasses on private land may additionally commit the offence of aggravated trespass contrary to ss. 68 and 69 of the Criminal Justice and Public Order Act 1994.

Many hunt protesters may restrict their activities to the public highway and may seek to exercise a perceived constitutional right of freedom of exercise over public highways. They may argue legitimate interests accordingly. However, in the recent case of *DPP* v *Jones and Another* (unreported), 23 January 1997, the Divisional Court held that the public's rights were limited to using the highway for the purpose of passing and re-passing, including any uses ancillary thereto which were usual and reasonable. Consequently, there is no established right in law to use the highway to hold a demonstration, however peaceful that demonstration may or may not be. Thus the hunt protesters' absence of a right to demonstrate over the public highway apparently contrasts with the rights of the hunt to pursue their prey over private land provided that they do so with the consent of the relevant landowners.

3.12   The media

This country has always afforded high regard to the freedom of the press to investigate and publish. This is in contrast to the right of the individual to privacy which has not been formally recognised. Any lawyer considering the conflict between the freedom of the press and the right to individual privacy must begin from the general point that there is no general common law right to privacy (although confidential relationships do exist which are entitled to the courts' protection, e.g., intimacies in a matrimonial relationship).

Once it is established that the plaintiff is, prima facie, being harassed by a journalist, the legitimate interests of the plaintiff and the journalist must be considered and the balance of interests test construed accordingly.

Does the plaintiff have a legitimate interest which is being infringed? It is most unlikely that this principle will apply to the publication of a true story which may be controversial or compromising, since publication of 'the truth' is always regarded as being in the public interest. Only the laws concerning libel or defamation can prevent such publication. However, the principle will be applied to protect the plaintiff against constant and oppressive journalistic interest which goes beyond publication of the truth in the public interest. This might relate to the unreasonableness of the behaviour meted out by the press, or to the fact that the story may have already broken and constant publication of a stale story to the detriment of a plaintiff might not, in the circumstances, be justifiable. Thus, Diana, Princess of Wales had little difficulty in obtaining an injunction against Martin Stenning who constantly followed her and adversely affected her quality of life over months rather than weeks, his intention being not to publish a story in the public interest but to obtain photographs of her in intimate circumstances (which were not necessarily offensive) and which were taken in the hope that such photographs would command large payments.

Nevertheless, the Princess has been severely criticised for the actions she committed on 31 March 1997 against the photographer Brendon Beirne. Beirne took photographs of her in Earls Court as she emerged from a gym. She sought to persuade him to surrender the film to her, and when he refused to do so voluntarily she enlisted the help of a male passer-by who grabbed Beirne's camera and removed the film. The Princess's actions — as a result of which Mr Beirne was assaulted and his film misappropriated — were clearly unlawful.

Mr Beirne's case illustrates the difficulties caused by the conflict between media personalities and press photographers. Prima facie such photographers are entitled to take reasonable and responsible photographs in public places. Such conduct cannot be regarded either as unreasonable or as likely to cause harassment. Aggravated features are required if harassment is to be established, and this will depend very much upon the particular facts, the confrontation itself and the history of the conduct of the respective parties. Clearly confrontation by a photographer who is known to be a trouble-maker and/or who seeks constantly to shadow a person is entirely different from occasional photography by a responsible photographer. The court might take the view that while acts of harassment had been committed, such acts were either justifiable or unactionable.

Does the defendant have a legitimate interest which he or she is entitled to protect? This similarly depends upon a consideration of the defendant's interests, the prima facie right to publish a true story of whatever nature, and the methods used by the journalists to investigate the story. Clearly more robust methods are justified when exposing criminal activities of convicted criminals than when exposing the marital indiscretions of a relatively unimportant public official. It is a question of degree in each particular case, and the respective rights and interests of the parties will need to be balanced accordingly. The credentials of the particular journalist/photographer and the bona fide nature of the investigation will also be taken into account.

In essence civil harassment is a conduct-based tort and the conduct of the respective parties, particularly that of the alleged harasser, will be salient.

3.13 Neighbourhood disputes

It is clear that a great deal of tension can exist between neighbours who may sometimes resort to campaigns of harassment. Most neighbour disputes are concerned with whether or not the actions of the allegedly harassing neighbour amount to harassment, and whether such behaviour adversely affects the quality of life of the alleged victim.

All neighbourhood disputes will need to be considered by reference to the basic principles which are as follows:

(a)   Is there cause for concern about the behaviour meted out by one neighbour to another?

(b)   Does such behaviour adversely affect the right of the injured neighbour to enjoy his or her property in a reasonable manner?

(c)   Does the allegedly harassing neighbour have a legitimate right to behave in a manner which may be detrimental to the allegedly injured neighbour?

Thus, neighbourhood disputes are similarly concerned with the principles of legitimate interests and the balance of interests test between the respective parties. Such interests may, of course, be construed under the law of nuisance.

Where behaviour is clearly (at best) anti-social or unreasonable, there will usually be no problem in defining it as 'harassing'. What is more difficult to deal with are the circumstances in which behaviour is, prima facie, legitimate — and indeed may be of vital importance to the interests of the particular neighbour. Thus a musician who works from home will undoubtedly wish to practise, and it is submitted that reasonable practice should not be construed as harassing behaviour, however annoying such activity might be. Once again, it will be a question of balancing the legitimate interests involved in listening to or playing music as against the legitimate interest in living a normal, peaceful life.

3.14   Northern Ireland

Section 13 of the Act provides for it to be extended to Northern Ireland. As is well known, the issue of marches is a particularly vexed question in the Province. Up to now, the problem has had to be resolved by the police using their public order powers. Under the Protection from Harassment Act 1997, where residents of an estate do not wish to have a particular march going through their area, they could perhaps apply to the courts for injunctions under s. 3 on the basis that an annual march constitutes a 'course of conduct' causing them harassment, alarm or distress. If the march went ahead the marchers would then be committing a criminal offence contrary to s. 3(6).

Chapter Four
Fear of Violence

4.1 Elements of the offence

When the Home Office proposals were announced to deal with stalking, two criminal offences were proposed — a 'lower level' offence and a 'higher level' offence. Section 2 deals with the proposed lower level offence, and s. 4 with the higher level offence.

4. Putting people in fear of violence

(1) A person whose course of conduct causes another to fear, on at least two occasions, that violence will be used against him is guilty of an offence if he knows or ought to know that his course of conduct will cause the other so to fear on each of those occasions.

As already discussed in relation to ss. 1 and 2, 'course of conduct' means conduct on at least two occasions (s. 7(3)) and 'conduct' includes speech (s. 7(4)). Also similar is the provision in s. 4(2) relating to the state of mind, the knowledge and the intention of the defendant:

(2) For the purposes of this section, the person whose course of conduct is in question ought to know that it will cause another to fear that violence will be used against him on any occasion if a reasonable person in possession of the same information would think the course of conduct would cause the other so to fear on that occasion.

(See s. 1(2) at 2.12.)

4.2 Punishment

Section 4 is an either-way offence punishable in the magistrates' court with up to six months' imprisonment, and/or a £5,000 fine and a restraining order (ss. 4(4)(b) and 5(1)) and punishable in the Crown Court with up to five years' imprisonment, an unlimited fine and a restraining order (ss. 4(4)(a) and 5(1)). Because an offence under s. 4 is punishable with up to five years' imprisonment, police have the power to arrest without warrant anyone they reasonably suspect of having committed the offence relying on their normal arrest powers under s. 24(6) of the Police and Criminal Evidence Act 1984.

4.3 Difficulties with the offence

Section 4(1) is an unfortunately worded provision in that it refers to 'a course of conduct' and then carries on to add 'on at least two occasions', thereby ignoring the fact that under s. 7(3) 'course of conduct' already means conduct on at least two occasions. It is arguable that this choice of words means that fear must be caused on at least four occasions. That is undoubtedly not what Parliament intended. However, in any criminal charge where there is ambivalence or uncertainty in the wording of a charge, the defendant should be given the benefit of that doubt, and clearly this charge is very poorly worded and is open to objection if only two incidents are alleged.

4.4 Application of the offence

It is difficult to see how this new offence adds to the already existing criminal law. Any words or actions which cause a victim to apprehend the immediate infliction of unlawful force already constitute the offence of common assault. Causing a person to fear immediate unlawful violence is an offence contrary to s. 4 of the Public Order Act 1986, and the use or threat of unlawful violence such as to cause a person of reasonable firmness to fear for his or her personal safety, is an offence contrary to s. 3 of the Public Order Act 1986.

The main value of s. 4 would appear to be to allow the courts to deal with serious stalking without having to wait until psychological or bodily harm is caused. However, it is likely that most of those cases will be dealt with at an earlier stage by prosecution under s. 2 of the Act combined with restraining orders. Nevertheless, there may be some — it is hoped few — cases of seriously threatening stalking for which prosecution under s. 4 will be appropriate.

Another possible use for the charge may be where somebody is in receipt of threats which are neither threats of immediate unlawful violence (s. 4, Public Order Act), nor threats to kill (s. 16, Offences Against the Person Act 1861), but which involve threats to commit harm of an unspecified nature, at an unspecified time and place. It might also be of use where threats are made over the telephone or by post which are considered too serious to be dealt with adequately under s. 43 of the Telecommunications Act 1984, or s. 1 of the Malicious Communications Act 1988 (see Appendix 4).

Although the offence under s. 4 adds very little to the already existing criminal law, it is possible that it may be a popular charge so far as the police are concerned, simply because of the possibility that a person convicted of an offence under s. 4 could be made the subject of a restraining order under s. 5 of the Act, discussed in more detail in chapter 5. For this reason, police may be inclined to charge breaches of s. 4 in circumstances where other charges are possibly more appropriate.

4.5 Alternative offences

As already discussed in relation to s. 2, the possibility of a restraining order being imposed on an offender under the Act may lead to complex plea bargaining, with lawyers who represent defendants charged with s. 4 offences offering pleas to other charges which do not carry the risk of a restraining order. If it is clear to defending lawyers that the prosecution are charging s. 4 only in order to obtain a restraining order then a likely tactic will be to offer to plea to a charge under s. 2 on the basis that the defendant will agree that a restraining order should be imposed by the court as part of the sentence.

Such an offer could be made in the Crown Court even though the s. 2 offence is triable summarily only. Under s. 4(5), in a Crown Court trial for an offence under s. 4 the jury may find the defendant guilty of a s. 2 offence even if they have found him not guilty of the s. 4 offence. The wording of that section is almost identical to the wording of s. 7(3) of the Public Order Act 1986 which applies when a defendant is being tried in the Crown Court for an offence contrary to ss. 2 or 3 of the Public Order Act. A jury in such a case are allowed to find the defendant not guilty of the serious charge but guilty of the summary only offence under s. 4 of the 1986 Act. It is common for defendants in the Crown Court to plead to s. 4 and for that plea to be accepted by the judge without any jury ever being empanelled. A similar pragmatic approach will probably be taken by the Crown Court in relation to pleas to s. 2 of the Protection from Harassment Act 1997. Whether by plea or by jury verdict, a Crown Court judge dealing with an offender under s. 2 has only the same sentencing powers as a magistrates' court (s. 4(6)).

Because the s. 4 offence has to be committed on at least two (arguably four) occasions, it will be vital for the prosecution to prove that there was a realistic fear of violence on each occasion complained of. It may well be argued that if no violence is actually used on the first occasion then, realistically speaking, on the subsequent occasion(s) there would be no real reason to fear that violence would actually be used. That problem, like the others, will have to be resolved by the courts in due course, and it remains to be seen whether s. 4 turns out to be a workable criminal offence in practice.

4.6 Defences

As with ss. 1, 2 and 3, there are specific defences to charges under s. 4 of the Act:

4. Putting people in fear of violence

(3) It is a defence for a person charged with an offence under this section to show that—

(a)   his course of conduct was pursued for the purpose of preventing or detecting crime,

(b)   his course of conduct was pursued under any enactment or rule of law or to comply with any condition or requirement imposed by any person under any enactment, or

(c)   the pursuit of his course of conduct was reasonable for the protection of himself or another or for the protection of his or another's property.

It should be noted that s. 4(3)(c) has different wording to the equivalent defence set out in s. 1(3)(c). Under s. 1(3)(c) it is sufficient for the defendant to show that in the particular circumstances the pursuit of the course of conduct was reasonable; in relation to s. 4 it is not sufficient for the defendant merely to claim that his actions were reasonable, they will have to be reasonable 'for the protection of himself or another or for the protection of his or another's property'. It is therefore a much more limited defence, which is probably understandable bearing in mind that a much more serious offence is being alleged. In practical terms, however, it is likely that defences offered to charges under s. 4 will be similar to defences to charges under s. 2.

Under s. 12 of the Act, where a Government minister certifies that any actions undertaken by a specified person on a specified occasion related to:

(a)   national security;

(b)   the economic well-being of the United Kingdom; or

(c)   the prevention or detection of serious crime;

and were done on behalf of the Crown the certificate is conclusive evidence that the Act does not apply to any conduct of that person on that occasion.

Chapter Five
Restraining Orders

Under s. 5 of the Act, where a person is convicted of an offence contrary to ss. 2 or 4, the court may make a restraining order to 'prohibit the defendant from doing anything described in the order'. Restraining orders are to be made:

> ... for the purpose of protecting the victim of the offence, or any other person mentioned in the order, from further conduct which —
> (a)   amounts to harassment, or
> (b)   will cause a fear of violence ... (s. 5(2))

Under s. 5(5): 'If without reasonable excuse the defendant does anything which he is prohibited from doing by an order under this section, he is guilty of an offence.'

Under s. 5(6), breach of any of the terms of a restraining order is made an either-way offence punishable in the magistrates' court with up to six months' imprisonment, or a £5,000 fine or both, and punishable in the Crown Court with up to five years' imprisonment, or an unlimited fine or both. Because breach of a restraining order is an offence punishable with up to five years' imprisonment, police can arrest without warrant anyone they reasonably suspect of having breached an order relying on their normal arrest powers under s. 24(6) of the Police and Criminal Evidence Act 1984.

5.1   Background to restraining orders

Criminal courts have always had limited powers to impose orders on convicted offenders. They have a historic power to bind over defendants to be of good behaviour and to keep the peace. In addition they have statutory powers to disqualify drivers from driving and to ban violent football supporters from attending football matches. However, breach of these orders has been punishable only with small fines or limited imprisonment, and therefore giving criminal courts the power to make orders, breach of which can be punished with up to five years' imprisonment, must be regarded as a completely new concept in the criminal law.

Criminal courts have been able to impose bail conditions for many years, and typical conditions have included staying away from witnesses, staying away from particular geographical areas and — particularly in the case of burglars and young offenders — staying at home during the hours of darkness. However, the fact that such bail conditions end once a defendant has been sentenced has often produced results which victims of crime have found difficult to understand. A defendant who claims to be innocent can be forbidden to contact someone whom he or she is alleged to have assaulted, but once convicted he or she is free to return to, speak to, and thereby cause fear and concern to the person whom he or she has been convicted of assaulting.

It has been recognised for many years that the absence of any power for criminal courts to control a defendant's behaviour post-conviction is a definite weakness in the criminal law. It is common to see horror stories in the press such as, 'Man Who Raped Me Now Lives Around the Corner'. These stories are often presented as if the victim is asking for the defendant to be returned to prison, but in reality quite often what victims are really asking is for the law to ensure that they never have to have contact again with the person who attacked them. In 'stalking' cases, where a defendant suffered from an obsession he would often continue to write to his victim from prison. Unless the victim obtained an injunction, or the letters were obscene or threatening, the prison authorities had no legal power to prevent the letters being sent despite the distress they were causing.

When Janet Anderson MP introduced her Private Member's Stalkers Bill into Parliament, it included a provision allowing criminal courts to make 'prohibitory orders' against offenders. The Government's original proposals to deal with stalking did not contain any equivalent provision, but following an article in the *Police Review*, 16 August 1996, the idea of giving criminal courts the power to make restraining orders was adopted by the Government and included in the 1997 Act.

5.2 Characteristics of restraining orders

It is perhaps unfortunate that restraining orders are restricted to convictions under ss. 2 and 4 of the Act. It is somewhat peculiar that a defendant who merely causes another to fear that violence will be used against him can be ordered not to contact his victim again, but someone who actually uses violence cannot be made subject to a similar order. However, if restraining orders prove to be effective, it is quite probable that in time they will be extended to cover other offences.

In considering restraining orders it is important to remember at the outset that they are creations of statute and therefore the law that applies to them is to be found completely within the wording of s. 5. Case law involving injunctions is not relevant and should not be relied on by lawyers either applying for or opposing restraining orders.

Though s. 5(2) allows courts to prohibit the defendant from 'doing anything described in the order', the purpose of the order must be to protect the victim of the offence, or any other person mentioned in the order, from further conduct which amounts to harassment or will cause a fear of violence. The behaviour forbidden by the order must therefore bear some relationship to the behaviour alleged in the criminal offence. It is likely that courts, particularly magistrates' courts, will impose conditions similar to those commonly imposed as bail conditions. Where a defendant pleads guilty it will be important for the defence and prosecution to be clear as to precisely what facts are agreed and what facts are in dispute. If there are disputes as to the facts then courts will probably have to hold a *Newton* hearing in order to determine the factual basis on which a restraining order can be based. (*R* v *Newton* (1982) 77 Cr App R 13 is discussed in detail in *Blackstone's Criminal Practice 1997*, paras D17.2–D17.13.)

5.3 Plea bargaining

The fact that restraining orders can be imposed only for offences contrary to the 1997 Act will put particular pressures on both prosecution and defence lawyers with regard to plea bargaining. Defence lawyers with clients charged with offences under the Act will have to consider offering pleas to other charges; while courts and prosecutors, when considering whether to accept such pleas, will have to take into account the fact that pleas to other charges will prevent the court making a restraining order.

In certain situations, however, defence lawyers may actively offer to plead to an offence under the Act in situations where a client is charged with a serious offence, such as an assault occasioning actual bodily harm, or a s. 3 offence under the Public Order Act 1986. In such cases defence lawyers might offer to plead at the magistrates' court to an offence contrary to s. 2 of the 1997 Act, on the basis that they would agree that the court should make a restraining order preventing any future contact with the injured party. In certain circumstances such an offer could well be an attractive option for the CPS, particularly in cases where there are vulnerable or easily frightened witnesses whose primary desire is to prevent any further repetition of the behaviour complained of.

Where defendants are charged with offences contrary to ss. 2 and 4, judges and magistrates are likely to be conscious of the possibility that they could make a restraining order. That fact may make them less willing to accept pleas to alternative charges unless the prosecution can satisfy them as to the reasons why alternative charges are being suggested. Both courts and prosecutors will have to take account of the fact that in many situations a plea to the summary only offence contrary to s. 2 of the Act, combined with a restraining order, may well be a more effective means of disposing of a case than proceeding with a more serious charge which cannot be dealt with by a restraining order. Careful calculation will be required in each case.

5.4 Applying for restraining orders

Another particular problem for prosecutors arises from the fact that restraining orders are part of the sentencing powers of the court, and therefore prosecutors have no actual right to ask the court to make a restraining order or to suggest what a restraining order should contain. In reality, however, courts, particularly magistrates' courts, will probably expect prosecutors to come prepared with typed draft orders for the court to consider. Prosecutors do have the right to remind the court of its power to make a restraining order and to ask the court if it would be of assistance if the prosecutor put forward some suggestions, and a court can ask a prosecutor if he or she has any suggestions which he or she would wish the court to consider. Defence lawyers, however, will have every right to object if a prosecutor attempts to apply for an order, or to suggest what its terms should be without being invited by the court to do so.

5.5   Making of restraining orders

Considering that breach of a restraining order is punishable with up to five years' imprisonment, it is astonishing that there are no provisions in the Act detailing the procedures to be followed by courts when making such orders; nor are there any provisions for the making of court rules or practice directions. This is in sharp contrast to the position relating to exclusion orders made under s. 30 of the Public Order Act 1986. Breach of such exclusion orders is punishable with only one month's imprisonment, but the Public Order Act still contains an entire section detailing the procedures to be followed by courts when making, revoking or varying such an order.

Even though no equivalent procedure is required under s. 5, it will probably be advisable for a court to discuss with the defendant and his legal representatives the terms of any order which the court is proposing to make and to allow the defendant and his legal representatives to comment on them. It will be advisable for the terms of the order to be typed up before the defendant leaves the court, and a copy given to the defendant. A copy of the order should also be provided to the police in the same way that the police are informed of bail conditions. A copy of the order signed by the judge, or by the chairman of the bench and the justices clerk, should also be kept on the court file and a record made in the court register of the fact that the defendant was physically handed a copy of the order. Following such a procedure would prevent any arguments being raised in the future as to whether or not the defendant was aware of the terms of the order.

Under s. 5(1), a restraining order can be made by a court in addition to any other sentence which it chooses to impose, and there is therefore no objection to a court sending a defendant to prison and at the same time making a restraining order. This may be sensible in several situations — for example, if a restraining order is in force prohibiting the defendant from contacting his victim again then that would give the prison authorities the power to prevent an obsessive defendant writing to his victim, and would also ensure the protection of the victim after the defendant has been released. A court making an order in such a case should of course ensure that the prison is provided with a copy of the restraining order.

5.6   Breach of restraining orders

Under s. 5(5): 'If without reasonable excuse the defendant does anything which he is prohibited from doing by an order under this section, he is guilty of an offence.' The crucial words in this provision are 'without reasonable excuse'. Whether a defendant had a reasonable excuse for any breach of a restraining order will be a matter of fact to be decided by the court of trial. For example, if a defendant is forbidden to enter a particular street and is a passenger in a car which travels down that street, he or she is unlikely to be in breach of a restraining order. If, however, he or she is constantly a passenger in a car which travels up and down that street, daily or hourly, then he or she could well be in breach of a restraining order, since there would be no reasonable excuse for not making alternative arrangements.

In order to secure a conviction under s. 5(5), the prosecution will need to prove both the actual terms of the order and the fact that the defendant knew of those terms. If the terms are unclear or ambiguous, or if there is any doubt as to whether the defendant knew what the terms were, then the defendant would have a reasonable excuse for any breach. Proving the terms of an order will require the prosecution to obtain a copy of the court register, certified in accordance with r. 68 of the Magistrates' Court Rules 1981 in the case of magistrates' court orders, and in accordance with s. 132 of the Supreme Court Act 1981 in the case of Crown Court orders.

5.7   Persistent offenders

Because the sentence for breach of a restraining order is potentially five years' imprisonment, such orders have the potential quite drastically to raise the stakes in respect of certain types of repetitive offences. For example, it is quite common to have situations on certain housing estates where gangs gather at night drinking, shouting obscenities at locals as they go by, and generally creating an intimidating or frightening atmosphere. Police powers to deal with such situations can often be somewhat limited unless they can obtain definite evidence that the youths have been engaged in criminal damage or violence of some kind. If any offence is committed it is usually only contrary to s. 5 of the Public Order Act 1986, by causing harassment, alarm or distress to members of the public and the local neighbours, and while the police have the power to arrest for that offence the only sentence the court can impose is a fine. If the gang returns the next night and repeat their behaviour, they once again are only committing an offence under s. 5 of the Public Order Act, and once again the courts are only able to impose a fine. If this situation continues for any period of time then there can be a growing air of lawlessness in the area, and a growing feeling of disillusionment amongst the neighbours at the inability of the police to deal with the situation. This conception that minor but repeated offences can have a significance to society out of all proportion to their legal status was the basis for the New York Police's 'Zero Tolerance' campaign which has now been adopted by several British police forces.

It is possible that the police will seek to use the potential of restraining orders as an integral part of this zero tolerance policing strategy. Looking at the above example again, on the first night the behaviour would still only breach s. 5 of the Public Order Act 1986, but if the behaviour was repeated the next night or for a number of nights then it would become a course of conduct contrary to s. 2 of the Protection from Harassment Act 1997. The offenders are now committing an imprisonable offence and the courts therefore have greater powers to deal with them, even though what is actually being done is no different from what was being done previously. Following conviction under s. 2 of the Act, the court could make a restraining order which might, for example, prohibit an offender from re-entering the estate, or prohibit gathering at a particular popular trouble spot. Other possibilities involve prohibiting the public drinking of alcohol or shouting insults at the local residents — in fact anything which can be logically defined as part of the offending behaviour which has constituted the course of conduct complained of. Breach of the terms of the order would be punishable by up to five years' imprisonment. In principle, therefore, repetitive minor public order offending could end up being dealt with severely by the courts. Some examples of possible restraining orders and their suggested format are set out in Appendix 7.

5.8   Juvenile offenders

Another characteristic of restraining orders which could be particularly significant, is the fact that they are not restricted with regard to the age of the offender. For all practical purposes it is impossible to obtain injunctions against young people under 18 years of age because civil courts are reluctant to use their contempt powers against juveniles. However, juveniles can be charged in the youth court with offences under the Protection from Harassment Act 1997, and there is nothing in the Act preventing youth courts making restraining orders as part of their normal sentencing powers. It is very probable that magistrates in the youth court will welcome the chance to make such orders.

A great deal of young offending can be defined as harassment because it is often confined to particular geographical areas and is often public-order based. Youth courts have been willing to use their power to impose bail conditions in order to control youngsters who are accused of imprisonable offences. Bail conditions which confine juveniles to their homes after 8 p.m. are commonly imposed by youth courts, as are conditions that they attend school regularly and do not go to particular geographical areas. Bail conditions are of course often broken by offenders, but the police have the power to arrest for any breach.

In view of their experience with such bail conditions, it is likely that youth courts will want to make restraining orders whenever feasible, quite possibly in very precise and Draconian terms, For example, if acts of harassment have been committed during school hours, it might be reasonable for a court to make a condition in a restraining order that the youngster should go to school every day, and should only be excused from attending school if ill at home. The police would then be able to monitor whether the juvenile obeyed the order, and if the juvenile offender stayed away from school he or she could be arrested for the offence of being in breach of a restraining order. Similarly, if the harassment occurred after the hours of darkness, it might be reasonable for a youth court to impose a restraining order requiring the young offender to be at home after a specified time.

Such possibilities are perhaps extreme but are quite possible. There have already been calls on various sides of the political fence for curfew orders to be imposed on youngsters generally, as has been done in certain American cities. Individual restraining orders with curfew conditions imposed on juveniles convicted of offences could prove to be a popular alternative to blanket youth curfew orders which would hit innocent and guilty youngsters alike. Certainly, the ability of restraining orders to deal with youngsters who would not be effectively dealt with by injunctions, is a point which should not be overlooked.

5.9   Private prosecutions

The existence of restraining orders may also encourage private prosecutions under the Act. In certain situations it may be considered — particularly by racial groups, neighbourhood groups etc. — that prosecution in the magistrates' court would be a more cost-effective way of curbing behaviour than going through the civil court injunction route. Where an injured party or group is eligible for legal aid, it would probably be more sensible to proceed via the civil court route. If legal aid is not available, though, then a private prosecution in the magistrates' court for offences contrary to s. 2 of the Act would be cheaper and quite possibly quicker.

As already indicated, where offenders are under the age of 18, proceeding by means of private prosecution in the youth court would be the only effective means of obtaining an order to prevent further harassing or anti-social behaviour. Neighbour-hood groups and racial groups have shown an increased willingness to club together and take legal action when necessary, and it could be that if they considered that the police or authorities were not taking effective action against harassing youngsters then private prosecution would be an option. If such a private prosecution was successful then the court could order that the prosecutor's legal costs should be paid out of central funds under s. 17 of the Prosecution of Offences Act 1985. There is the additional advantage that if a private prosecution is successful and a restraining order is granted, it is likely that the police will be more inclined to enforce it than they would an injunction granted under s. 3 of the Act. As discussed in chapter 6, it is probable that where injunctions have been granted, the police and the CPS will take the view that contempt proceedings are the appropriate way of dealing with any breach. With restraining orders, however, there is no alternative to the order being enforced through the criminal courts, and therefore both the police and the CPS are likely to feel obliged to enforce any restraining order which has been granted by the criminal courts even if the order was granted as a result of a private prosecution.

5.10   Varying or discharging an order

Under s. 5(3), a restraining order may be made for a specific period or 'until further order'. Under s. 5(4), 'The prosecutor, the defendant or any other person mentioned in the order may apply to the court which made the order for it to be varied or discharged by a further order'. Even though there are no time-limits specified in the

Act, it is likely that magistrates' courts will not wish to make restraining orders for periods of more than two years, particularly orders applying to young offenders. If a defendant applies to vary an order and is refused, there is no time-limit specified before a further application to vary is made. Courts would probably be justified in refusing to hear a further application until a reasonable time — such as three or six months — has passed. While it is not explicitly set out in the Act, it would seem that any refusal to vary an order could be appealed from the magistrates' court to the Crown Court. Where the order was originally made by the Crown Court, any application to vary or discharge must be made to the Crown Court not the magistrates' court.

Chapter Six
Breach of an Harassment Injunction

6.1 Background

When stalking became a political and media issue in 1996, it quickly became apparent that one of the main perceived inadequacies in the law was the inability of the police to arrest stalkers who had breached civil court injunctions ordering them not to contact or go near their victims again. The civil courts were showing a willingness to grant injunctions prohibiting harassing or stalking behaviour, but the obsessive mentality of many stalkers meant that they frequently breached such injunctions causing further stress and harm to their victims.

When the police were contacted by the victims of such stalking, the officers involved felt understandably frustrated at their own inability to take any action to enforce the injunction, while the victims regarded the lack of police enforcement as leaving them unprotected by the law, so making the injunction meaningless. Breach of a civil court injunction is of course punishable with imprisonment as a contempt of court, but police officers have no general power to arrest for breach of injunctions. The civil courts contempt procedure is somewhat complex and slow, and victims who did not qualify for legal aid were having to bear the costs personally.

In the consultation process undertaken by the Home Office prior to the 1997 Act it became apparent that this problem had to be addressed. The simplest solution to the problem would have been to allow the civil courts to attach a power of arrest to harassment injunctions in the same way that a power of arrest can be attached to domestic violence injunctions granted under s. 3 of the Domestic Violence and Matrimonial Proceedings Act 1976. Adopting the same procedure for harassment injunctions would have been simple, straightforward and effective, and it is difficult to understand why the Government did not adopt this course instead of introducing the bizarre, unprecedented and probably unworkable idea of making breach of the civil court injunction a criminal offence.

6.2 The criminal offence

3. Civil remedy
(6)   Where —

(a)　the High Court or a county court grants an injunction for the purpose mentioned in subsection (3)(a), and

(b)　without reasonable excuse the defendant does anything which he is prohibited from doing by the injunction,

he is guilty of an offence.

The criminal offence created by s. 3(6) is an either-way offence punishable in the magistrates' court with up to six months' imprisonment, and/or a £5,000 fine (s. 3(9)(b)) and punishable in the Crown Court with up to five years' imprisonment and/or an unlimited fine (s. 3(9)(a)). Because the offence is punishable with up to five years' imprisonment, police officers have the power to arrest without warrant anyone they reasonably suspect of having committed the offence relying on their normal arrest powers under s. 24(6) of the Police and Criminal Evidence Act 1984. The police therefore have been given an indirect rather than a direct power to arrest for breach of civil court non-harassment injunctions.

6.3　Problems with the criminal offence

This indirect approach is riddled with practical problems which were clearly not properly thought out when the legislation was drafted. It seems to have been assumed, in Parliament and by the Home Office, that the police would arrest an offender for the criminal offence of breach of the injunction contrary to s. 3(6), and would then decide whether to charge the offender with the criminal offence or bring him before the civil courts to be dealt with under the normal contempt of court procedure. However, the police have not been given the necessary powers for this to happen. If a police officer arrests a defendant under s. 3(6) then the defendant is being arrested solely for a criminal offence, not for breach of an injunction, and therefore has to be dealt with in accordance with criminal (not civil) procedure. The only powers the police have are to charge the defendant with the criminal offence or release him, unlike the situation under the Domestic Violence and Matrimonial Proceedings Act 1976 where the police are given the express power to arrest a defendant who breaches a non-molestation injunction and then bring him before a judge. The only way in which a defendant can be arrested and brought before a civil court to be dealt with for breaching a non-harassment injunction is if the victim goes back to court and obtains an arrest warrant under the procedure laid down in s. 3(3) to (5). The police have no power to initiate contempt proceedings, which remain the responsibility of the person who obtained the injunction.

Under s. 3(7) and (8), breach of an anti-harassment injunction may be punished either by being dealt with as a criminal offence, or by being dealt with as a contempt of court. The two options are expressed so as to be mutually exclusive:

(7)　Where a person is convicted of an offence under subsection (6) in respect of any conduct, that conduct is not punishable as a contempt of court.

(8)　A person cannot be convicted of an offence under subsection (6) in respect of any conduct which has been punished as a contempt of court.

While the Act makes it clear that a defendant convicted of the criminal offence of breaching the injunction cannot then be dealt with for civil contempt, and a defendant dealt with for contempt cannot then be convicted of the criminal offence, the position is unclear with regard to a defendant who has been charged with the criminal offence and is awaiting trial. During that time can he or she be dealt with for contempt, or are contempt proceedings held in abeyance pending the outcome of the criminal proceedings? What is the position if the victim wishes to proceed by way of the contempt procedure but the police and CPS wish to proceed with the criminal charge? Also (and probably more likely), what is the position if the police have charged the offender and the CPS consider that the breach of the injunction could best be dealt with by the contempt procedure? What if the CPS discontinue the prosecution because they consider that there is insufficient evidence, or that there is no public interest in proceeding? Lastly, what is the position regarding a defendant who has been tried for the criminal offence and acquitted?

As the Act is worded, it would seem that where a defendant is tried for the criminal offence and acquitted there is nothing to prevent his or her being proceeded against for contempt. This places a defendant in the unenviable position of being in double jeopardy, which flies in the face of general principles of fairness in legal proceedings and is arguably in breach of Article 4.1 of Protocol 7 of the European Convention of Human Rights. It is to be hoped that courts would regard any attempt to institute contempt proceedings following an unsuccessful criminal trial as an abuse of process, but the possibility has not been clearly dealt with in the Act.

It is uncertain what the attitude of the CPS and the judiciary will be towards prosecutions brought under s. 3(6). Unless the breach of the injunction is extremely serious, Crown prosecutors will probably take the view that there is no public interest in proceeding with a prosecution and that any breach should be dealt with as a contempt. Judges in the Crown Court are also likely to question why the prosecution are proceeding by way of a criminal charge instead of the more straightforward contempt procedure. The only circumstances in which it is likely that criminal proceedings rather than contempt proceedings would be justified are likely to be where the harassment is bizarre and it is clear that the offender needs psychiatric treatment or an order under the Mental Health Act, neither of which can be ordered by a civil court dealing with contempt of court proceedings.

6.4 Undertakings

There is a further problem created by the way s. 3(6) is worded. Under s. 3(6)(a), the criminal offence occurs only in situations where 'the High Court or a county court grants an injunction'. It is common in civil proceedings for applications for injunctions to be disposed of by the defendant giving 'undertakings' to the court. Undertakings are a promise to the court, and as such, if the undertakings are broken, the defendant can be proceeded against for contempt of court. However, a court accepting undertakings given by a defendant is not the same thing as a court granting an injunction.

In the case of *Carpenter* v *Carpenter* [1988] 1 FLR 121, Bingham LJ (as he was then) held that under the Domestic Violence and Matrimonial Proceedings Act 1976, a power of arrest could not be attached to undertakings because the wording of the Act referred to 'injunctions' and undertakings are not the same as injunctions.

It is a basic rule of criminal law that all criminal statutes are interpreted restrictively and that any ambiguities are interpreted in favour of the defendant. Because the offence created by s. 3(6) is of an unprecedented nature, this will further tend to favour a restricted and literal interpretation being given to the wording of the section. In the absence of any specific wording in the Act to the contrary and applying the principles in *Carpenter* v *Carpenter* it seems certain that breach of undertakings will not be a criminal offence under s. 3(6) but will only be a contempt of court.

This puts the police in a difficult position. Individual officers could easily find themselves in situations where they are told that a non-harassment injunction has been granted, and they therefore arrest for the offence of breaching the injunction. If it subsequently transpires that no injunction has in fact been granted, then it is possible that the police may be liable to be sued for unlawful arrest. Under s. 24(6) of the Police and Criminal Evidence Act 1984, a police officer may arrest anyone whom he 'has reasonable grounds for suspecting' has committed an arrestable offence. However, on what basis does a police officer form 'reasonable grounds to suspect' that someone has breached an injunction? It is after all a unique power of arrest, and therefore police officers who arrest solely on the basis of what they are told could potentially be held not to have reasonable grounds for the arrest. In order for there to be reasonable grounds for an arrest the arresting officer would need to be shown the injunction so as to be satisfied that it exists and to consider what its terms are. Alternatively, the arresting officer would need to confirm with police records that there is such an injunction. In effect this would require non-harassment injunctions to be registered with the police. The potential problems surrounding s. 3(6) will probably make the police reluctant to arrest for breach of non-harassment injunctions, and they may consider that it would be safer to tell the harassed person that he or she should return to court and institute contempt proceedings against the harasser — the very problem the Act was supposed to solve!

This does not mean that the police are completely powerless where an injunction is allegedly breached. Where a police officer is told that a particular person is harassing someone and is also informed that the person is subject to an injunction, the police officer will have reasonable grounds to suspect that the particular person has committed an offence contrary to s. 2 because there will be an alleged repetition of previous behaviour constituting the necessary course of conduct required for an arrest under s. 2. Once back in the police station the police officer could then make full enquiries to determine whether an injunction actually exists, what its terms are and whether an offence under s. 3(6) has actually been committed. If a police officer was to arrest under s. 3(6) and it subsequently transpired that there was no injunction the arrest would not be made lawful merely because the police officer could have arrested under s. 2. In *DPP* v *Maudling* (unreported), 4 December 1996 (see *Police Review*, 14 February 1997), it was decided that where a police officer made an unlawful arrest, the fact that other valid arrest powers existed could not make the arrest lawful. If a police officer is assaulted while making an unlawful arrest the defendant will not be guilty of assaulting the police officer in the execution of his duty.

If, despite these difficulties, a prosecution is commenced under s. 3(6) then the prosecution will need to prove that an injunction was granted and its terms. This will be done by producing a sealed copy of it in the case of a High Court injunction (ord. 38, r. 10(2), Rules of the Supreme Court 1965), or a certified copy in the case of a county court injunction (s. 12, County Courts Act 1984). The prosecution will have to establish that the defendant had 'no reasonable excuse' for breaching the injunction. If the defendant claims that he did have a reasonable excuse then in certain circumstances, particularly in a jury trial, that could involve going over the circumstances and the evidence given when the injunction was granted.

There is one final problem arising from the wording of s. 3(3)(a): it refers to 'an injunction for the purpose of restraining the defendant from pursuing any conduct which amounts to harassment'. Using the word 'any' could imply that s. 3(6) is not restricted to injunctions granted under the Protection from Harassment Act 1997, but could apply to any injunction which involves any form of protection from harassment. However, s. 3(3)(a) begins with the words 'in such proceedings' which is a clear reference to s. 3(1), and it is therefore likely that the courts will interpret s. 3(6) as only applying to injunctions which are clearly and unambiguously made under s. 3.

The fact that the Act makes breach of a non-harassment injunction a criminal offence could have an unfortunate inhibiting effect on the willingness of the civil courts to make such injunctions. Civil court judges will undoubtedly be urged by defence lawyers to grant these injunctions only if satisfied about the allegations beyond reasonable doubt, rather than applying the normal civil tests of the balance of probabilities and the balance of convenience. It would be ironic if the effect of the Act was actually to make it harder rather than easier for harassed persons to obtain injunctions.

Overall, s. 3(6) is an unfortunately worded section, and is based on the false philosophy that civil and criminal law can be muddled with impunity. Since the Act gives criminal courts the power to grant restraining orders following criminal conviction, there is little, if any, justification whatsoever for the provisions of s. 3(6); it is likely that in practice police officers and the CPS will consider it better to confine themselves to dealing with the 'normal' criminal offences under ss. 2, 4 and 5, and leave the enforcement of civil injunctions to be dealt with by the civil rather than the criminal courts. What is impossible to predict is whether the victims of harassment may be tempted to use s. 3(6) as the basis for private prosecutions as an alternative to contempt proceedings.

6.5 Civil procedure: arrest warrant

In addition to creating a criminal offence of breach of an injunction granted under s. 3, the Act creates a new procedure allowing the civil courts to issue an arrest warrant following such a breach.

Under s. 3(3)(b), where the plaintiff considers that the defendant has done anything which he is prohibited from doing by the injunction, the plaintiff may apply for the issue of a warrant for the arrest of the defendant.

The application for such a warrant must be made to a High Court judge in the case of a High Court injunction, or to a judge or district judge in the case of a county court injunction. The application is made *ex parte*, and must ordinarily be supported by affidavit evidence, though the Act contemplates oral sworn evidence as s. 3(5)(a) states that 'the application is substantiated on oath'. The injunction must restrain the defendant from pursuing any conduct which amounts to harassment, and it is clear that the cause of action must be framed under the statutory tort of harassment provided for by s. 3(1).

The judge or district judge may order the issue of a warrant for the arrest of the defendant if there are reasonable grounds for believing that 'the defendant has done anything which he is prohibited from doing by the injunction' (s. 3(5)(b)).

The Act does not specify the procedure for dealing with the defendant once he has been arrested and brought before the civil courts, but presumably the normal civil contempt procedure will be adopted. It is noteworthy that the Act does not confer upon a civil judge the power to attach a power of arrest to any injunction ordered under s. 3(3), and therefore the procedure under s. 3(3) is an *ex post facto* procedure which does nothing to deter a defendant from breaching the injunction in the first place. This means that illogically the civil policing of harassment injunctions will be different from that of domestic violence injunctions and injunctions generally.

As already discussed above, undertakings are not the same as injunctions even though both can be punished as a contempt. Consequently a warrant cannot be issued under s. 3(3) if the defendant has given undertakings to avoid an injunction (*Carpenter* v *Carpenter* [1988] 1 FLR 121).

6.6   The terms of the injunction

The general law concerning the granting of injunctions is contained in s. 37 of the Supreme Court Act 1981:

37.   Powers of High Court with respect to injunctions and receivers

(1)   The High Court may by order (whether interlocutory or final) grant an injunction . . . in all cases in which it appears to the court to be just and convenient to do so.

(2)   Any such order may be made either unconditionally or on such terms and conditions as the court thinks just.

This provision applies to the county courts under s. 38 of the County Courts Act 1984.

Thus, in order to obtain an interlocutory injunction, the plaintiff must establish a good, arguable case under the statutory tort of harassment (s. 3(1)), and that it is 'just and convenient' for the court to order such an injunction.

It is submitted that under s. 37(1) of the 1981 Act the plaintiff has to satisfy a relatively low threshold, although it is clear that injunctions will be awarded only if the interests of justice are served.

When considering whether and upon what terms to order an injunction, the court will apply the principle of legitimate interests and the balance of interests test between the parties. The court will need to consider which interests or series of interests take priority and whether, in order to protect the legitimate interests of the plaintiff, it is necessary to restrict the interests of the alleged harasser.

An ordinary injunction under the statutory tort will probably include, *inter alia*, provisions preventing the defendant from:

(a)   assaulting, molesting, harassing, threatening, pestering or otherwise interfering with the plaintiff;

(b)   making any communication to the plaintiff, whether in writing or orally, whether by telephone or otherwise, save that the defendant may send written communications to the plaintiff's solicitors; and

(c)   coming or remaining within a certain distance of the plaintiff's home address or the plaintiff's place of work.

Item (c) above is normally referred to as the exclusion zone order, and the extent of the exclusion zone will depend upon the relevant geography and the relevant facts. A wider exclusion zone will normally be ordered in a country area, and a narrower one in a large, built-up area. The operation of an exclusion zone will be difficult if, for instance, the parties live in the same street, or have places of work in proximity to each other. If this is the case, the court may require an exclusion zone to be referenced to a scaled plan which would prohibit the defendant coming within specified areas, or even a particular street. Specimen particulars of claim limited to injunctive relief and a draft order are set out in Appendix 6.

It is clear that a civil defendant may be the subject of a civil injunction even though his or her actions may have been, prima facie, lawful. Indeed the wording of s. 3(1) enables the court to provide injunctive relief even when the defendant has not yet committed a wrongful act since the sub-clause 'may be the victim' contemplates pre-emptive injunctive relief to deter a potential harasser or even to protect a potential victim. However, a course of conduct or threatened course of conduct would normally have to be proved because the injunctive relief is in respect of harassing behaviour prohibited in s. 1.

A number of cardinal principles arise which are fundamental to the manner in which the civil courts award injunctive relief:

(a)   *The need to protect a victim from an aggressor is paramount:* ... 'respect for the freedom of the aggressor should never lead the court to deny necessary protection to the victim.' (*per* Sir Thomas Bingham MR in *Burris* v *Azadani*, at p. 811)

(b)   *The civil courts will restrain lawful behaviour in order to protect a plaintiff's legitimate interests:* '... it would not seem to me to be a valid objection to the making of an [injunctive] order that the conduct to be restrained is not in itself tortious or otherwise unlawful if such an order is reasonably regarded as necessary for the protection of a plaintiff's legitimate interests.' (*per* Sir Thomas Bingham MR in *Burris* v *Azadani*, at p. 807)

This is not a new principle, but it is a principle which will become more widely used as the law of harassment develops. The *quia timet* injunction is an illustration of this. It was used in *Khorasandjian* v *Bush* [1993] 3 All ER 669. The following *dictum* is relevant: 'the court is entitled to look at the defendant's conduct as a whole and restrain, on a *quia timet* basis, also those aspects of his campaign of harassment which cannot strictly be classified as threats' (*per* Dillon LJ in *Khorasandjian* v *Bush*, at p. 677). Thus, prima facie, behaviour which falls short of threatening or harassing behaviour can be the subject of injunctive relief.

(c)   *The civil courts will adopt a balance of interests test in order to reconcile the respective interests of the victim and the aggressor:* The interests of the aggressor 'must be respected up to the point at which his conduct infringes, or threatens to infringe, the rights of the plaintiff' (*per* Sir Thomas Bingham MR in *Burris* v *Azadani*, at p. 810)

What is significant is that a defendant may be in the unhappy position of being charged with breaching a civil injunction which was imposed even though he or she had done nothing unlawful up to the point of imposition of the injunction.

(d)   *The conduct of the parties to the injunction:* An illustration of the kind of conduct which can breach an injunction, and typifies the classic harasser or stalker, is that of Azadani in *Burris* v *Azadani*. Azadani and his servants or agents were ordered not to assault, molest, harass, threaten, pester or otherwise interfere with Mrs Burris and her infant children. He was prevented from communicating with her or her children, whether in writing or by telephone, save by written communication to her solicitors. He was prevented from coming or remaining within 250 yards of her home in South London.

At first instance, on 12 July 1995, Azadani received a total of 84 days' imprisonment for eight findings of contempt, which it is useful to set out as follows:

(i)   On 18 December 1994, his sister arrived at the plaintiff's home to have a discussion (breach 1 as she was clearly his agent).

(ii)   On 26 December 1994, one of the defendant's friends arrived at the plaintiff's address to deliver a cassette tape and Christmas cards from him (breach 2).

(iii)   In January 1995, he left a message on her telephone answering machine (breach 3).

(iv)   On 1 February 1995, he left a message on her telephone answering machine (breach 4).

(v)   On 2 February 1995, he posted an envelope through her letter-box (finding of trespass — breach 5).

(vi)   On 4 April 1995, he knocked at her front door. He placed a note through her letter-box and left parcels for the plaintiff's children (finding of trespass — breach 6).

(vii)   On 6 July 1995, he cycled past the plaintiff's home (breach 7).
(viii)   On 7 July 1995, he cycled past the plaintiff's house (breach 8).

On review, the Court of Appeal reduced the term of imprisonment to 28 days and reimposed a suspended term of 56 days which had been activated by the first instance judge. The grounds for the reduction were the mitigating circumstances flowing from the fact that while Azadani had breached the order and was therefore guilty of contempt, he had not directly aimed his behaviour at the plaintiff: the last two incidents were limited to bicycling past her house.

The contempt perpetrated by Azadani and the manner in which the Court of Appeal considered the original sentence of the trial judge should provide helpful guidance to the courts when dealing with breach of an injunction issued under s. 3.

6.7   The past course of harassment

It has already been established that a defendant does not necessarily have to have committed a course of harassment to be the subject of an injunction. It is sufficient if a course of harassment has been threatened or is feared. An injunction can be ordered if it is considered that the plaintiff's legitimate interests are being or might be infringed by the defendant's behaviour. Consequently, it is possible for a defendant to breach an injunction even though he or she has not yet committed an unlawful act other than the breach itself.

6.8   Breach of undertaking

The procedures and possible penalties for breaching an undertaking are different to those for breaches of an injunction. Lawyers representing a plaintiff who claims that an undertaking has been breached may seek to persuade the civil court to replace the undertaking with an injunction and not to make any findings for contempt. This may be difficult as it is not up to a party to withdraw contempt proceedings. Contempt proceedings are technically matters to be dealt with by the civil court. If for any reason contempt proceedings are instituted and the court does make findings of contempt, it may be that s. 3(8) will not apply if the court (unusually) declines to punish the defendant for such contempt. The absence of punishment would possibly leave open the option of a criminal charge under s. 3(6), though defence lawyers in such circumstances would undoubtedly argue that the defendant is being placed in double jeopardy. This may not prove to be such a difficult problem in practice, but there are undoubted pitfalls, and both civil and criminal lawyers will need to be aware of any proceedings taking place in the other court.

6.9   Local authority/police injunctions

As discussed above, the police may in general be reluctant to become involved in enforcing s. 3 injunctions taken out by private individuals. However, it is possible that they may seek to use such injunctions themselves to control regular offenders, neighbourhood harassers or frequent protesters.

Neither the police nor the CPS have any power to apply for injunctions preventing anticipated or actual criminal behaviour. The Attorney-General does have such a power allowing him to apply for any injunction by means of a 'relator action', but this power is usually only used in exceptional cases. For example, in December 1996 a newly released prisoner, David Jennings, was alleged to have said that he was going to 'Do a Dunblane', i.e., attack children in school. The Attorney-General successfully applied for an injunction preventing Jennings entering or going near school premises. Because any such application requires the personal approval of the Attorney-General it is not a procedure which is used frequently.

However, under s. 222 of the Local Government Act 1972 local councils have the power to apply for injunctions where they 'consider it expedient for the promotion or protection of the inhabitants of their area'. In *Stoke on Trent City Council* v *B&Q (Retail) Ltd* [1984] 2 All ER 332, the House of Lords decided that this provision entitles local councils to apply for injunctions to prevent actual or anticipated criminal acts in their area. Local councils have made extensive use of this power to deal with minor but repetitive offenders, particularly unlicensed street traders and prostitutes leaving 'calling cards' in telephone boxes. They have not, however, used it to deal with more serious offenders since most injunctions do not carry any power of arrest and so are of little value to the police.

The fact that the police can both arrest and charge for breach of anti-harassment injunctions could lead police and local councils to co-operate to obtain injunctions under s. 3, restraining the activities of known offenders and gangs whose behaviour is causing harassment to the inhabitants of the local area. The police would provide the evidence from records of conviction and other intelligence in their possession, and would be able to enforce the injunctions by arrest and prosecution under s. 3(6). Though s. 3(1) refers to proceedings being brought by 'the victim of the course of conduct', a local council could claim to be acting on behalf of a number of victims resident within its area.

A strategy of using injunctions enforced by the police has been successfully implemented by the local authorities in San Jose and Los Angeles County, and was endorsed by the California Supreme Court in *People ex rel Gallo* v *Acuna* 14 cal 4th 1090 (1997). These injunctions are primarily aimed at 'gangs' and include conditions that named gang members should not associate together, should not enter particular neighbourhoods and should not drink alcohol in public.

In Britain police and local councils are increasingly working together to deal with crime and anti-social behaviour. It would be suprising if they ignored the possibility of using s. 3 injunctions as a further weapon in their legal armoury.

Appendix 1
Protection from Harassment Act 1997

CHAPTER 40
ARRANGEMENT OF SECTIONS

England and Wales

Protection from Harassment Act 1997

1997 CHAPTER 40

An Act to make provision for protecting persons from harassment and similar conduct. [21st March 1997]

BE IT ENACTED by the Queen's most Excellent Majesty, by and with the advice and consent of the Lords Spiritual and Temporal, and Commons, in this present Parliament assembled, and by the authority of the same, as follows:—

England and Wales

1. Prohibition of harassment

(1) A person must not pursue a course of conduct—

(a) which amounts to harassment of another, and

(b) which he knows or ought to know amounts to harassment of the other.

(2) For the purposes of this section, the person whose course of conduct is in question ought to know that it amounts to harassment of another if a reasonable person in possession of the same information would think the course of conduct amounted to harassment of the other.

(3) Subsection (1) does not apply to a course of conduct if the person who pursued it shows—

(a) that it was pursued for the purpose of preventing or detecting crime,

(b) that it was pursued under any enactment or rule of law or to comply with any condition or requirement imposed by any person under any enactment, or

(c) that in the particular circumstances the pursuit of the course of conduct was reasonable.

2. Offence of harassment

(1) A person who pursues a course of conduct in breach of section 1 is guilty of an offence.

(2) A person guilty of an offence under this section is liable on summary conviction to imprisonment for a term not exceeding six months, or a fine not exceeding level 5 on the standard scale, or both.

(3)   In section 24(2) of the Police and Criminal Evidence Act 1984 (arrestable offences), after paragraph (m) there is inserted—

'(n)   an offence under section 2 of the Protection from Harassment Act 1997 (harassment).'.

3.   Civil remedy

(1)   An actual or apprehended breach of section 1 may be the subject of a claim in civil proceedings by the person who is or may be the victim of the course of conduct in question.

(2)   On such a claim, damages may be awarded for (among other things) any anxiety caused by the harassment and any financial loss resulting from the harassment.

(3)   Where—

(a)   in such proceedings the High Court or a county court grants an injunction for the purpose of restraining the defendant from pursuing any conduct which amounts to harassment, and

(b)   the plaintiff considers that the defendant has done anything which he is prohibited from doing by the injunction,

the plaintiff may apply for the issue of a warrant for the arrest of the defendant.

(4)   An application under subsection (3) may be made—

(a)   where the injunction was granted by the High Court, to a judge of that court, and

(b)   where the injunction was granted by a county court, to a judge or district judge of that or any other county court.

(5)   The judge or district judge to whom an application under subsection (3) is made may only issue a warrant if—

(a)   the application is substantiated on oath, and

(b)   the judge or district judge has reasonable grounds for believing that the defendant has done anything which he is prohibited from doing by the injunction.

(6)   Where—

(a)   the High Court or a county court grants an injunction for the purpose mentioned in subsection (3)(a), and

(b)   without reasonable excuse the defendant does anything which he is prohibited from doing by the injunction,

he is guilty of an offence.

(7)   Where a person is convicted of an offence under subsection (6) in respect of any conduct, that conduct is not punishable as a contempt of court.

(8)   A person cannot be convicted of an offence under subsection (6) in respect of any conduct which has been punished as a contempt of court.

(9)   A person guilty of an offence under subsection (6) is liable—

(a)   on conviction on indictment, to imprisonment for a term not exceeding five years, or a fine, or both, or

(b)   on summary conviction, to imprisonment for a term not exceeding six months, or a fine not exceeding the statutory maximum, or both.

4. Putting people in fear of violence

(1)   A person whose course of conduct causes another to fear, on at least two occasions, that violence will be used against him is guilty of an offence if he knows or ought to know that his course of conduct will cause the other so to fear on each of those occasions.

(2)   For the purposes of this section, the person whose course of conduct is in question ought to know that it will cause another to fear that violence will be used against him on any occasion if a reasonable person in possession of the same information would think the course of conduct would cause the other so to fear on that occasion.

(3)   It is a defence for a person charged with an offence under this section to show that—

(a)   his course of conduct was pursued for the purpose of preventing or detecting crime,

(b)   his course of conduct was pursued under any enactment or rule of law or to comply with any condition or requirement imposed by any person under any enactment, or

(c)   the pursuit of his course of conduct was reasonable for the protection of himself or another or for the protection of his or another's property.

(4)   A person guilty of an offence under this section is liable—

(a)   on conviction on indictment, to imprisonment for a term not exceeding five years, or a fine, or both, or

(b)   on summary conviction, to imprisonment for a term not exceeding six months, or a fine not exceeding the statutory maximum, or both.

(5)   If on the trial on indictment of a person charged with an offence under this section the jury find him not guilty of the offence charged, they may find him guilty of an offence under section 2.

(6)   The Crown Court has the same powers and duties in relation to a person who is by virtue of subsection (5) convicted before it of an offence under section 2 as a magistrates' court would have on convicting him of the offence.

5. Restraining orders

(1)   A court sentencing or otherwise dealing with a person ('the defendant') convicted of an offence under section 2 or 4 may (as well as sentencing him or dealing with him in any other way) make an order under this section.

(2)   The order may, for the purpose of protecting the victim of the offence, or any other person mentioned in the order, from further conduct which—

(a)   amounts to harassment, or

(b)   will cause a fear of violence,

prohibit the defendant from doing anything described in the order.

(3)   The order may have effect for a specified period or until further order.

(4)   The prosecutor, the defendant or any other person mentioned in the order may apply to the court which made the order for it to be varied or discharged by a further order.

(5) If without reasonable excuse the defendant does anything which he is prohibited from doing by an order under this section, he is guilty of an offence.

(6) A person guilty of an offence under this section is liable—

(a) on conviction on indictment, to imprisonment for a term not exceeding five years, or a fine, or both, or

(b) on summary conviction, to imprisonment for a term not exceeding six months, or a fine not exceeding the statutory maximum, or both.

6. Limitation

In section 11 of the Limitation Act 1980 (special time limit for actions in respect of personal injuries), after subsection (1) there is inserted—

'(1A)   This section does not apply to any action brought for damages under section 3 of the Protection from Harassment Act 1997.'

7. Interpretation of this group of sections

(1)   This section applies for the interpretation of sections 1 to 5.

(2)   References to harassing a person include alarming the person or causing the person distress.

(3)   A 'course of conduct' must involve conduct on at least two occasions.

(4)   'Conduct' includes speech.

Scotland

8. Harassment

(1)   Every individual has a right to be free from harassment and, accordingly, a person must not pursue a course of conduct which amounts to harassment of another and—

(a)   is intended to amount to harassment of that person; or

(b)   occurs in circumstances where it would appear to a reasonable person that it would amount to harassment of that person.

(2)   An actual or apprehended breach of subsection (1) may be the subject of a claim in civil proceedings by the person who is or may be the victim of the course of conduct in question; and any such claim shall be known as an action of harassment.

(3)   For the purposes of this section—

'conduct' includes speech;

'harassment' of a person includes causing the person alarm or distress; and a course of conduct must involve conduct on at least two occasions.

(4)   It shall be a defence to any action of harassment to show that the course of conduct complained of—

(a)   was authorised by, under or by virtue of any enactment or rule of law;

(b)   was pursued for the purpose of preventing or detecting crime; or

(c)   was, in the particular circumstances, reasonable.

(5)   In an action of harassment the court may, without prejudice to any other remedies which it may grant—

(a)   award damages;

(b)   grant—

(i)   interdict or interim interdict;

(ii)   if it is satisfied that it is appropriate for it to do so in order to protect the person from further harassment, an order, to be known as a 'non-harassment order', requiring the defender to refrain from such conduct in relation to the pursuer as may be specified in the order for such period (which includes an indeterminate period) as may be so specified,

but a person may not be subjected to the same prohibitions in an interdict or interim interdict and a non-harassment order at the same time.

(6)   The damages which may be awarded in an action of harassment include damages for any anxiety caused by the harassment and any financial loss resulting from it.

(7)   Without prejudice to any right to seek review of any interlocutor, a person against whom a non-harassment order has been made, or the person for whose protection the order was made, may apply to the court by which the order was made for revocation of or a variation of the order and, on any such application, the court may revoke the order or vary it in such manner as it considers appropriate.

(8)   In section 10(1) of the Damages (Scotland) Act 1976 (interpretation), in the definition of 'personal injuries', after 'to reputation' there is inserted ', or injury resulting from harassment actionable under section 8 of the Protection from Harassment Act 1997'.

9.   Breach of non-harassment order

(1)   Any person who is found to be in breach of a non-harassment order made under section 8 is guilty of an offence and liable—

(a)   on conviction on indictment, to imprisonment for a term not exceeding five years or to a fine, or to both such imprisonment and such fine; and

(b)   on summary conviction, to imprisonment for a period not exceeding six months or to a fine not exceeding the statutory maximum, or to both such imprisonment and such fine.

(2)   A breach of a non-harassment order shall not be punishable other than in accordance with subsection (1).

10.   Limitation

(1)   After section 18A of the Prescription and Limitation (Scotland) Act 1973 there is inserted the following section—

18B.   Actions of harassment

(1)   This section applies to actions of harassment (within the meaning of section 8 of the Protection from Harassment Act 1997) which include a claim for damages.

(2)   Subject to subsection (3) below and to section 19A of this Act, no action to which this section applies shall be brought unless it is commenced within a period of 3 years after—

(a)   the date on which the alleged harassment ceased; or

(b)   the date (if later than the date mentioned in paragraph (a) above) on which the pursuer in the action became, or on which, in the opinion of the court, it would have been reasonably practicable for him in all the circumstances to have become, aware, that the defender was a person responsible for the alleged harassment or the employer or principal of such a person.

(3)   In the computation of the period specified in subsection (2) above there shall be disregarded any time during which the person who is alleged to have suffered the harassment was under legal disability by reason of nonage or unsoundness of mind.

(2)   In subsection (1) of section 19A of that Act (power of court to override time-limits), for 'section 17 or section 18 and section 18A' there is substituted 'section 17, 18, 18A or 18B'.

11.   Non-harassment order following criminal offence

After section 234 of the Criminal Procedure (Scotland) Act 1995 there is inserted the following section—

234A.   Non-harassment orders

(1)   Where a person is convicted of an offence involving harassment of a person ('the victim'), the prosecutor may apply to the court to make a non-harassment order against the offender requiring him to refrain from such conduct in relation to the victim as may be specified in the order for such period (which includes an indeterminate period) as may be so specified, in addition to any other disposal which may be made in relation to the offence.

(2)   On an application under subsection (1) above the court may, if it is satisfied on a balance of probabilities that it is appropriate to do so in order to protect the victim from further harassment, make a non-harassment order.

(3)   A non-harassment order made by a criminal court shall be taken to be a sentence for the purposes of any appeal and, for the purposes of this subsection 'order' includes any variation or revocation of such an order made under subsection (6) below.

(4)   Any person who is found to be in breach of a non-harassment order shall be guilty of an offence and liable—

(a)   on conviction on indictment, to imprisonment for a term not exceeding 5 years or to a fine, or to both such imprisonment and such fine; and

(b)   on summary conviction, to imprisonment for a period not exceeding 6 months or to a fine not exceeding the statutory maximum, or to both such imprisonment and such fine.

(5)   The Lord Advocate, in solemn proceedings, and the prosecutor, in summary proceedings, may appeal to the High Court against any decision by a court to refuse an application under subsection (1) above; and on any such appeal the High Court may make such order as it considers appropriate.

(6)   The person against whom a non-harassment order is made, or the prosecutor at whose instance the order is made, may apply to the court which made the order for its revocation or variation and, in relation to any such

application the court concerned may, if it is satisfied on a balance of probabilities that it is appropriate to do so, revoke the order or vary it in such manner as it thinks fit, but not so as to increase the period for which the order is to run.

(7)   For the purposes of this section 'harassment' shall be construed in accordance with section 8 of the Protection from Harassment Act 1997.

General

12.   National security, etc.

(1)   If the Secretary of State certifies that in his opinion anything done by a specified person on a specified occasion related to—

(a)   national security,

(b)   the economic well-being of the United Kingdom, or

(c)   the prevention or detection of serious crime,

and was done on behalf of the Crown, the certificate is conclusive evidence that this Act does not apply to any conduct of that person on that occasion.

(2)   In subsection (1), 'specified' means specified in the certificate in question.

(3)   A document purporting to be a certificate under subsection (1) is to be received in evidence and, unless the contrary is proved, be treated as being such a certificate.

13.   Corresponding provision for Northern Ireland

An Order in Council made under paragraph 1(1)(b) of Schedule 1 to the Northern Ireland Act 1974 which contains a statement that it is made only for purposes corresponding to those of sections 1 to 7 and 12 of this Act—

(a)   shall not be subject to sub-paragraphs (4) and (5) of paragraph 1 of that Schedule (affirmative resolution of both Houses of Parliament), but

(b)   shall be subject to annulment in pursuance of a resolution of either House of Parliament.

14.   Extent

(1)   Sections 1 to 7 extend to England and Wales only.

(2)   Sections 8 to 11 extend to Scotland only.

(3)   This Act (except section 13) does not extend to Northern Ireland.

15.   Commencement

(1)   Sections 1, 2, 4, 5 and 7 to 12 are to come into force on such day as the Secretary of State may by order made by statutory instrument appoint.

(2)   Sections 3 and 6 are to come into force on such day as the Lord Chancellor may by order made by statutory instrument appoint.

(3)   Different days may be appointed under this section for different purposes.

16.   Short title

This Act may be cited as the Protection from Harassment Act 1997.

Appendix 2
Principles Applying to the Civil Tort of Harassment

Burris v *Azadani* [1995] 4 All ER 802.

1. Harassment is a PRIMARY tort.
2. Civil courts have power to restrain lawful behaviour.
3. Lawful behaviour will be restrained in order to protect a plaintiff's legitimate interests.
4. The need to protect a victim from aggression/harassment is paramount.
5. The civil courts will adopt a balance of interests test in order to reconcile the respective interests of the victim and the aggressor/harasser.
6. The civil courts will impose interlocutory injunctions using the normal tests:

    (a)   arguable cause of action.

    (b)   where it appears to the court 'to be just and convenient' (Supreme Court Act 1981, s. 37(1)).

7. The civil courts may protect a plaintiff's 'legitimate interests' even though such interests may fall outside the conventional terms of a cause of action in strict law.
8. The civil courts will concentrate on balancing the respective interests of the parties and not necessarily on the legal rights or wrongs of the behaviour with which they are concerned.

Appendix 3
Major Criminal Cases in 1996

CONVICTIONS

R v *Burstow* (1996) *The Times,* 30 July (psychological assault)

Principles:

(a)   An assault can be inflicted without the application of direct physical force.
(b)   The definition of grievous bodily harm includes psychological injury.
(c)   A campaign of non-physical harassment which causes psychological harm can constitute 'psychological assault'.

R v *Ireland* (1996) *The Times,* 22 May (telephone assault)

Principles:

(a)   A telephone call or a series of calls can constitute assault.
(b)   The calls have to place victims in immediate fear of their safety with resulting psychological injury. Merely causing fear, distress or pain is insufficient.
(c)   In order to establish assault, psychological injury resulting from the telephone call must be proved.

R v *Johnston* (1996) *The Times,* 22 May (telephone/public nuisance)

Principles:

(a)   Johnston made obscene telephone calls on hundreds of occasions to at least 13 different women in the South Cumbria area.
(b)   This was held to be conduct constituting a public nuisance since it materially affected 'a section of the public'.

ACQUITTALS

January 1996 — *Quinn* — Liverpool Magistrates' Court — 'Stalks the Princess Royal' — not guilty of behaviour likely to cause a breach of the peace — not bound over — actions were peaceful

March 1996 — *Wagner* — Horseferry Road Magistrates' Court — 'Stalks the Queen and Diana, Princess of Wales' — not guilty of behaviour likely to cause a breach of the peace — not bound over — actions peaceful

March 1996 — *Wilson* — Horseferry Road Magistrates' Court — harassed Charlotte Sell for many years — not guilty of intentional harassment

September 1996 — *Chambers* — Inner London Crown Court — campaign of harassment against Margaret Bent — not guilty of psychological assault (GBH) — no evidence of intention to cause psychological injury despite possession of a knife and a machete (on several occasions)

Appendix 4
Other Criminal Offences Involving Harassment

There is a large number of other criminal Acts which apply to offences of harassment in one form or another, and these are detailed in this Appendix. Commission of any of these offences on more than one occasion involving the same injured party would constitute harassment as defined in ss. 1 to 3 of the 1997 Act, and therefore repeated behaviour contrary to any of these Acts could be dealt with either by criminal conviction contrary to s. 2, or by means of an injunction under s. 3 of the 1997 Act.

It is quite possible that in cases where the prosecution could rely on one or more of these offences, they will prefer to charge the defendant with criminal harassment in the hope of obtaining a restraining order as well as a conviction. It is also likely that in most cases where criminal charges are laid for contravention of ss. 2 or 4 of the Act, alternative pleas could be offered using one or another of these offences. Almost all prosecutions brought under s. 4 of the Act could probably be dealt with by the offences of threats to kill or affray, or under s. 4 of the Public Order Act 1986, all of which are detailed below.

For convenience, where an offence is discussed in the current (1997) issue of *Blackstone's Criminal Practice*, the appropriate paragraph and page reference is provided.

Harassment, alarm and distress (B11.63, p. 482)

Public Order Act 1986, s. 5

5.—(1)   A person is guilty of an offence if he—

(a)   uses threatening, abusive or insulting words or behaviour, or disorderly behaviour, or

(b)   displays any writing, sign or other visible representation which is threatening, abusive or insulting,

within the hearing or sight of a person likely to be caused harassment, alarm or distress thereby.

(2)   An offence under this section may be committed in a public or a private place, except that no offence is committed where the words or behaviour are used, or the

writing, sign or other visible representation is displayed, by a person inside a dwelling and the other person is also inside that or another dwelling.

(3) It is a defence for the accused to prove—

(a) that he had no reason to believe that there was any person within hearing or sight who was likely to be caused harassment, alarm or distress, or

(b) that he was inside a dwelling and had no reason to believe that the words or behaviour used, or the writing, sign or other visible representation displayed, would be heard or seen by a person outside that or any other dwelling, or

(c) that his conduct was reasonable.

(4) A constable may arrest a person without warrant if—

(a) he engages in offensive conduct which a constable warns him to stop, and

(b) he engages in further offensive conduct immediately or shortly after the warning.

(5) In subsection (4) 'offensive conduct' means conduct the constable reasonably suspects to constitute an offence under this section, and the conduct mentioned in paragraph (a) and the further conduct need not be of the same nature.

(6) A person guilty of an offence under this section is liable on summary conviction to a fine not exceeding level 3 on the standard scale.

Fear or provocation of violence (B11.45, p. 478)

Public Order Act 1986, s. 4

4.—(1) A person is guilty of an offence if he—

(a) uses towards another person threatening, abusive or insulting words or behaviour, or

(b) distributes or displays to another person any writing, sign or other visible representation which is threatening, abusive or insulting,

with intent to cause that person to believe that immediate unlawful violence will be used against him or another by any person, or to provoke the immediate use of unlawful violence by that person or another, or whereby that person is likely to believe that such violence will be used or it is likely that such violence will be provoked.

(2) An offence under this section may be committed in a public or a private place, except that no offence is committed where the words or behaviour are used, or the writing, sign or other visible representation is distributed or displayed, by a person inside a dwelling and the other person is also inside that or another dwelling.

(3) A constable may arrest without warrant anyone he reasonably suspects is committing an offence under this section.

(4) A person guilty of an offence under this section is liable on summary conviction to imprisonment for a term not exceeding 6 months or a fine not exceeding level 5 on the standard scale or both.

Intentional harassment, alarm and distress (B11.55, p. 481)

Public Order Act 1986, s. 4A

4A.—(1) A person is guilty of an offence if, with intent to cause a person harassment, alarm or distress, he—

(a)   uses threatening, abusive or insulting words or behaviour, or disorderly behaviour, or

(b)   displays any writing, sign or other visible representation which is threatening, abusive or insulting,

thereby causing that or another person harassment, alarm or distress.

(2)   An offence under this section may be committed in a public or a private place, except that no offence is committed where the words or behaviour are used, or the writing, sign or other visible representation is displayed, by a person inside a dwelling and the person who is harassed, alarmed or distressed is also inside that or another dwelling.

(3)   It is a defence for the accused to prove—

(a)   that he was inside a dwelling and had no reason to believe that the words or behaviour used, or the writing, sign or other visible representation displayed, would be heard or seen by a person outside that or any other dwelling, or

(b)   that his conduct was reasonable.

(4)   A constable may arrest without warrant anyone he reasonably suspects is committing an offence under this section.

(5)   A person guilty of an offence under this section is liable on summary conviction to imprisonment for a term not exceeding 6 months or a fine not exceeding level 5 on the standard scale or both.

Affray (B11.37, p. 475)

Public Order Act 1986, s. 3

3.—(1) A person is guilty of affray if he uses or threatens unlawful violence towards another and his conduct is such as would cause a person of reasonable firmness present at the scene to fear for his personal safety.

(2)   Where 2 or more persons use or threaten the unlawful violence, it is the conduct of them taken together that must be considered for the purposes of subsection (1).

(3)   For the purposes of this section a threat cannot be made by the use of words alone.

(4)   No person of reasonable firmness need actually be, or be likely to be, present at the scene.

(5)   Affray may be committed in private as well as in public places.

(6)   A constable may arrest without warrant anyone he reasonably suspects is committing affray.

(7) A person guilty of affray is liable on conviction on indictment to imprisonment for a term not exceeding 3 years or a fine or both, or on summary conviction to imprisonment for a term not exceeding 6 months or a fine not exceeding the statutory maximum or both.

Threats to kill (B1.94, p. 138)

Offences Against the Person Act 1861, s. 16

16. A person who without lawful excuse makes to another a threat, intending that that other would fear it would be carried out, to kill that other or a third person shall be guilty of an offence and liable on conviction on indictment to imprisonment for a term not exceeding ten years.

Threats to cause criminal damage (B8.25, p. 401)

Criminal Damage Act 1971, s. 2

2. A person who without lawful excuse makes to another a threat, intending that that other would fear it would be carried out—
    (a) to destroy or damage any property belonging to that other or a third person; or
    (b) to destroy or damage his own property in a way which he knows is likely to endanger the life of that other or a third person;
shall be guilty of an offence.

Malicious telephone calls (B19.40, p. 669)

Telecommunications Act 1984, s. 43

43.—(1) A person who—
    (a) sends, by means of a public telecommunication system, a message or other matter that is grossly offensive or of an indecent, obscene or menacing character; or
    (b) sends by those means, for the purpose of causing annoyance, inconvenience or needless anxiety to another, a meassage that he knows to be false or persistently makes use for that purpose of a public telecommunication system,
shall be guilty of an offence and liable on summary conviction to imprisonment for a term not exceeding six months or a fine not exceeding level 5 on the standard scale or both.
    (2) Subsection (1) above does not apply to anything done in the course of providing a programme service (within the meaning of the Broadcasting Act 1990).

Malicious postal letters (B19.41, p. 669)

Malicious Communications Act 1988, s. 1

1.—(1)   Any person who sends to another person—
(a)   a letter or other article which conveys—
(i)   a message which is indecent or grossly offensive;
(ii)   a threat; or
(iii)   information which is false and known or believed to be false by the sender; or
(b)   any other article which is, in whole or part, of an indecent or grossly offensive nature,
is guilty of an offence if his purpose, or one of his purposes, in sending it is that it should, so far as falling within paragraph (a) or (b) above, cause distress or anxiety to the recipient or to any other person to whom he intends that it or its contents or nature should be communicated.

(2)   A person is not guilty of an offence by virtue of subsection (1)(a)(ii) above if he shows—
(a)   that the threat was used to reinforce a demand which he believed he had reasonable grounds for making; and
(b)   that he believed that the use of the threat was a proper means of reinforcing the demand.

(3)   In this section references to sending include references to delivering and to causing to be sent or delivered and 'sender' shall be construed accordingly.

(4)   A person guilty of an offence under this section shall be liable on summary conviction to a fine not exceeding level 4 on the standard scale.

Harassment during trade disputes (B11.102, p. 492)

Trade Union and Labour Relations (Consolidation) Act 1992, s. 241

241.—(1)   A person commits an offence who, with a view to compelling another person to abstain from doing or to do any act which that person has a legal right to do or abstain from doing, wrongfully and without legal authority—
(a)   uses violence to or intimidates that person or his wife or children, or injures his property,
(b)   persistently follows that person about from place to place,
(c)   hides any tools, clothes or other property owned or used by that person, or deprives him of or hinders him in the use thereof,
(d)   watches or besets the house or other place where that person resides, works, carries on business or happens to be, or the approach to any such house or place, or
(e)   follows that person with two or more other persons in a disorderly manner in or through any street or road.

(2)   A person guilty of an offence under this section is liable on summary conviction to imprisonment for a term not exceeding six months or a fine not exceeding level 5 on the standard scale, or both.

(3)   A constable may arrest without warrant anyone he reasonably suspects is committing an offence under this section.

Aggravated trespass (B13.42, p. 566) .

Criminal Justice and Public Order Act 1994, s. 68

68.—(1)   A person commits the offence of aggravated trespass if he trespasses on land in the open air and, in relation to any lawful activity which persons are engaging in or are about to engage in on that or adjoining land in the open air, does there anything which is intended by him to have the effect—

(a)   of intimidating those persons or any of them so as to deter them or any of them from engaging in that activity,

(b)   of obstructing that activity, or

(c)   of disrupting that activity.

(2)   Activity on any occasion on the part of a person or persons on land is 'lawful' for the purposes of this section if he or they may engage in the activity on the land on that occasion without committing an offence or trespassing on the land.

(3)   A person guilty of an offence under this section is liable on summary conviction to imprisonment for a term not exceeding three months or a fine not exceeding level 4 on the standard scale, or both.

(4)   A constable in uniform who reasonably suspects that a person is committing an offence under this section may arrest him without a warrant.

(5)   In this section 'land' does not include—

(a)   the highways and roads excluded from the application of section 61 by paragraph (b) of the definition of 'land' in subsection (9) of that section; or

(b)   a road within the meaning of the Roads (Northern Ireland) Order 1993.

Harassment of debtors (B5.85, p. 317)

Administration of Justice Act 1970, s. 40

40.—(1)   A person commits an offence if, with the object of coercing another person to pay money claimed from the other as a debt due under a contract, he—

(a)   harasses the other with demands for payment which, in respect of their frequency or the manner or occasion of making any such demand, or of any threat or publicity by which any demand is accompanied, are calculated to subject him or members of his family or household to alarm, distress or humiliation;

(b)   falsely represents, in relation to the money claimed, that criminal proceedings lie for failure to pay it;

(c)   falsely represents himself to be authorised in some official capacity to claim or enforce payment; or

  (d) utters a document falsely represented by him to have some official character or purporting to have some official character which he knows it has not.

(2) A person may be guilty of an offence by virtue of subsection (1)(a) above if he concerts with others in the taking of such action as is described in that paragraph, notwithstanding that his own course of conduct does not by itself amount to harassment.

(3) Subsection (1)(a) above does not apply to anything done by a person which is reasonable (and otherwise permissible in law) for the purpose—

  (a) of securing the discharge of an obligation due, or believed by him to be due, to himself or to persons for whom he acts, or protecting himself or them from future loss; or

  (b) of the enforcement of any liability by legal process.

(4) A person guilty of an offence under this section shall be liable on summary conviction to a fine of not more than level 5 on the standard scale.

Harassment of tenants (B13.1, p. 555)

Protection from Eviction Act 1971, s. 1

1.—(1) In this section 'residential occupier', in relation to any premises, means a person occupying the premises as a residence, whether under a contract or by virtue of any enactment or rule of law giving him the right to remain in occupation or restricting the right of any other person to recover possession of the premises.

(2) If any person unlawfully deprives the residential occupier of any premises of his occupation of the premises or any part thereof, or attempts to do so, he shall be guilty of an offence unless he proves that he believed, and had reasonable cause to believe, that the residential occupier had ceased to reside in the premises.

(3) If any person with intent to cause the residential occupier of any premises—

  (a) to give up the occupation of the premises or any part thereof; or

  (b) to refrain from exercising any right or pursuing any remedy in respect of the premises or part thereof;

does acts likely to interfere with the peace or comfort of the residential occupier or members of his household, or persistently withdraws or withholds services reasonably required for the occupation of the premises as a residence, he shall be guilty of an offence.

(3A) Subject to subsection (3B) below, the landlord of a residential occupier or an agent of the landlord shall be guilty of an offence if—

  (a) he does acts likely to interfere with the peace or comfort of the residential occupier or members of his household, or

  (b) he persistently withdraws or withholds services reasonably required for the occupation of the premises in question as a residence,

and (in either case) he knows, or has reasonable cause to believe, that that conduct is likely to cause the residential occupier to give up the occupation of the whole or part of the premises or to refrain from exercising any right or pursuing any remedy in respect of the whole or part of the premises.

(3B) A person shall not be guilty of an offence under subsection (3A) above if he proves that he had reasonable grounds for doing the acts or withdrawing or withholding the services in question.

(3C) In subsection (3A) above 'landlord', in relation to a residential occupier of any premises, means the person who, but for—

(a) the residential occupier's right to remain in occupation of the premises, or

(b) a restriction on the person's right to recover possession of the premises,

would be entitled to occupation of the premises and any superior landlord under whom that person derives title.

(4) A person guilty of an offence under this section shall be liable—

(a) on summary conviction, to a fine not exceeding the statutory maximum or to imprisonment for a term not exceeding 6 months or to both;

(b) on conviction on indictment, to a fine or to imprisonment for a term not exceeding 2 years or to both.

(5) Nothing in this section shall be taken to prejudice any liability or remedy to which a person guilty of an offence thereunder may be subject in civil proceedings.

(6) Where an offence under this section committed by a body corporate is proved to have been committed with the consent or connivance of, or to be attributable to any neglect on the part of, any director, manager or secretary or other similar officer of the body corporate or any person who was purporting to act in any capacity, he as well as the body corporate shall be guilty of that offence and shall be liable to be proceeded against and punished accordingly.

Statutory nuisances (noise etc.)

Environmental Protection Act 1990, ss. 79–80A

(These provisions are lengthy and complex therefore only s. 79(1) is reproduced here.)

79.—(1) Subject to subsections (2) to (6A) below, the following matters constitute 'statutory nuisances' for the purposes of this Part, that is to say—

(a) any premises in such a state as to be prejudicial to health or a nuisance;

(b) smoke emitted from premises so as to be prejudicial to health or a nuisance;

(c) fumes or gases emitted from premises so as to be prejudicial to health or a nuisance;

(d) any dust, steam, smell or other effluvia arising on industrial, trade or business premises and being prejudicial to health or a nuisance;

(e) any accumulation or deposit which is prejudicial to health or a nuisance;

(f) any animal kept in such a place or manner as to be prejudicial to health or a nuisance;

(g) noise emitted from premises so as to be prejudicial to health or a nuisance;

(ga)   noise that is prejudicial to health or a nuisance and is emitted from or caused by a vehicle, machinery or equipment in a street;

(h)   any other matter declared by any enactment to be a statutory nuisance; and it shall be the duty of every local authority to cause its area to be inspected from time to time to detect any statutory nuisances which ought to be dealt with under section 80 below or sections 80 and 80A below and, where a complaint of a statutory nuisance is made to it by a person living within its area, to take such steps as are reasonably practicable to investigate the complaint.

Breach of the peace (bind overs) (E11.1, p. 1738)

Magistrates' Courts Act 1980, s. 115

115.—(1)   The power of a magistrates' court on the complaint of any person to adjudge any other person to enter into a recognisance, with or without sureties, to keep the peace or to be of good behaviour towards the complainant shall be exercised by order on complaint.

(2)   Where a complaint is made under this section, the power of the court to remand the defendant under subsection (5) of section 55 above shall not be subject to the restrictions imposed by subsection (6) of that section.

(3)   If any person ordered by a magistrates' court under subsection (1) above to enter into a recognisance, with or without sureties, to keep the peace or to be of good behaviour fails to comply with the order, the court may commit him to custody for a period not exceeding 6 months or until he sooner complies with the order.

Appendix 5
Checklists Whether Act Applies

Checklist A: Where harassment is suspected

(1)   Is there evidence that a specific person has already been harassed, alarmed or distressed by the words or actions of another?
No — There is no criminal offence under the Act, but there may be civil proceedings if there are reasonable grounds to believe that harassment may occur in the future.
Yes — There may be a criminal offence under the Act or possible civil proceedings.

(2)   Has this person been harassed, alarmed or distressed on more than one occasion?
No — There is no criminal offence under the Act though other criminal offences may have been committed. There may be civil proceedings if there are reasonable grounds to believe that harassment may occur again.
Yes — Both criminal charges and civil proceedings are possible under the Act.

(3)   Even though the person has been harassed, alarmed or distressed on more than one occasion, can the words or actions which caused the harassment, alarm or distress be described in the ordinary use of language as a course of conduct, or are they in reality just separate, isolated incidents? Are the words or actions complained of similar on each occasion, are they closely linked in time, do they demonstrate common characteristics?
No — to all the above, then there is probably insufficient evidence for criminal charges but civil proceedings are possible.
Yes — to any of the above, then both criminal charges and civil proceedings are possible.

(4)   Even though a victim has been harassed, alarmed or distressed, can it be shown that the person who harassed, alarmed, or distressed him or her knew or ought to have known that that behaviour would have this effect? Are the words or actions complained of clearly and obviously words or actions which would cause harassment, alarm or distress? Are they insults, abuse, catcalls, or references of a personal,

defamatory or insulting nature? Has property been stolen, damaged or interfered with? Have threats been made to harm someone or to harm a pet? Have there been threats to damage or steal property?

No — Then next paragraph may apply.

Yes — Both criminal charges or civil proceedings are possible under the Act.

(5)   If the actions alleged are not clearly or obviously by their nature harassing, are there circumstances which show that the alleged harasser knew or ought to have known that what he or she was doing or saying amounted to harassment or would cause alarm or distress? Would a reasonable person in possession of the same information as the alleged harasser realise that the words or actions complained of would amount to harassment? Is there any evidence that the alleged harasser has said or done anything which indicates that he or she knew that his or her words or actions were causing harassment, alarm or distress? Is there any evidence that the alleged harasser was asked by the victim to stop his or her actions and refused to do so, or was the harasser told by a relative or close friend of the victim the effect that the actions were having, or told by a person in authority such as a policeman or a doctor?

No — Criminal charges are unlikely to succeed, though civil proceedings may succeed because of the lower standard of proof.

Yes — Then there is sufficient evidence to justify either criminal charges or civil proceedings.

Checklist B: Choosing between criminal prosecution and civil proceedings

(1)   Is the alleged harasser over 18 years of age or under 18 years of age?

Over 18 — Both civil proceedings and criminal prosecution are possible.

Under 18 — In practical terms, only criminal prosecution is available.

(2)   Is there clear evidence of harassment, or is the evidence unclear, problematical or ambiguous?

Evidence clear — Both civil proceedings and criminal prosecution are possible.

Evidence unclear or ambiguous — Civil proceedings are preferable because of the lower standard of proof.

(3)   Is there evidence of harassment having occurred on at least two occasions, or has there merely been harassment in the past on one occasion and fear that it will happen again?

If two occasions — Both civil proceedings and criminal charges are possible.

If only once and fear of repetition — Only civil proceedings are available.

(4)   Is the primary intention to punish the harasser, or to prevent future conduct by him?

To punish — Criminal proceedings would be necessary.

To prevent future conduct — Both civil and criminal proceedings are possible.

(5) Are the police charging the harasser with an offence under the Act?

Yes — Civil proceedings likely to be unnecessary because a criminal court may make a restraining order following conviction.

No — See next paragraph.

(6) Are the police charging the harasser with some other offence which involves the alleged incidents of harassment?

Yes — Civil proceedings will be necessary because a criminal court will not have power to make a restraining order following conviction for any offence other than an offence contrary to ss. 2 or 4 of the Act. A private prosecution under the Act would be unlikely to be allowed to proceed if it is based on incidents which have already been dealt with by other charges.

No — Both private prosecution or civil proceedings may be possible.

(7) Has the person already been charged with criminal harassment or another criminal offence, and has the charge been discontinued by the CPS?

Yes — Civil proceedings are the safest option. A private prosecution may be taken over by the CPS and discontinued if they consider that a prosecution is not in the public interest, but the CPS cannot intervene in civil proceedings.

No — Both private prosecution or civil proceedings may be possible.

(8) Is the victim of harassment eligible for legal aid?

Yes — Civil proceedings are recommended because legal aid can be granted to apply for an injunction but there is no legal aid for private prosecutions.

No — A private prosecution in the magistrates' court is likely to be cheaper than applying for an injunction in the county court, and the magistrates may make a restraining order against the harasser following conviction. However, there is no guarantee that they will do so.

Appendix 6
Specimen Particulars of Claim and Injunctions for Civil Proceedings under Section 3

Case no:

IN THE RODDENBERRY COUNTY COURT

KIRA NERYS   Plaintiff

— and —

EELAM GAREK   Defendant

PARTICULARS OF CLAIM
---

1. The Plaintiff claims Harassment under the terms of the Protection from Harassment Act 1997, full particulars of [the] allegations against the Defendant being contained in her affidavit dated   filed herein and served herewith, which affidavit the Plaintiff intends to stand as if the said particulars were pleaded herein.

2. The Plaintiff limits her claim for relief in these proceedings to Orders and directions pursuant to, inter alia, s. 3(3) Protection from Harassment Act 1997 AND FURTHER at the trial of this action to such orders as were exactly within the terms of the ex parte Order dated   which provided that:—

   (a)   'the Defendant be restrained and an injunction is hereby granted restraining the Defendant whether by himself, his servants or agents or any of them or otherwise howsoever from:—

   (i)   assaulting, molesting, harassing, threatening, pestering or otherwise interfering with the Plaintiff by doing acts to cause her harm whether directly or indirectly;

(ii)   making any communication to the Plaintiff whether in writing or orally, whether by telephone or otherwise howsoever save that he may send written communcation to the Plaintiff's solicitors;

(iii)   coming or remaining within [250] yards of the Plaintiff's home address of 1701-D Enterprise Road'

Served etc.

BY Messrs Worf, Quark & Dukat
    9 DS Towers
    Roddenberry

TO the Court in duplicate AND to the Defendant in person

Case no:

IN THE RODDENBERRY COUNTY COURT
BETWEEN:—

KIRA NERYS   Plaintiff

— and —

EELAM GAREK   Defendant

---

draft EX PARTE ORDER
(Under s. 3 Protection from Harassment Act 1997)

UPON hearing the Solicitor for the Plaintiff
AND UPON reading the affidavit of KIRA NERYS dated

AND UPON the Plaintiff, by his solicitor undertaking to abide by any Order that the Court may make as to damages in case the Court shall hereafter be of the opinion that the Defendant shall have sustained loss by reason of this Order which the Plaintiff ought to pay:

IT IS ORDERED and directed:

(1)   That the Defendant be restrained and an injunction is hereby granted pursuant to s. 3 Protection from Harassment Act 1997 restraining the Defendant whether by himself, his servants or agents or any of them, or otherwise howsoever from:—

(a)   assaulting, molesting, harassing, threatening, pestering or otherwise interfering with the Plaintiff by doing acts to cause her harm whether directly or indirectly;

(b)   making any communication to the Plaintiff whether in writing or orally, whether by telephone or otherwise howsoever save that he may send written communcation to the Plaintiff's solicitors;

(c)   coming or remaining within [250] yards of the Plaintiff's home address of 1701-D Enterprise Road until after the trial of this action or further Order.

(2)   That the Defendant shall have liberty to apply for a discharge or variation of this Order on 7 days' prior written notice in the meantime.

(3)   That the costs of this application be reserved [and that there be Legal Aid Taxation of the Plaintiff's costs].

Dated etc.

Appendix 7
Specimen Restraining Orders under Section 5

(I) RODDENBERRY MAGISTRATES' COURT
RESTRAINING ORDER

On

THE DEFENDANT James Tiberius Kirk

was convicted by this court of an offence contrary to s. 2(1) Protection from Harassment Act 1997 and the court made the following restraining order against the defendant under the provisions of s. 5(1) Protection from Harassment Act 1997.

1) THE DEFENDANT IS PROHIBITED from making any contact either directly or indirectly with Jadzia Dax.

2) THE DEFENDANT IS PROHIBITED from entering the street known as Enterprise Crescent or from driving along it. However the defendant may walk or drive along the street twice a day on his way to work or his way back from work but he may not stop, dawdle or talk to anyone whilst travelling along Enterprise Crescent.

3) THE DEFENDANT IS PROHIBITED from telephoning, writing, or sending E-mail to No. 1701 Enterprise Crescent the home of Jadzia Dax and her parents.

THIS ORDER SHALL EXPIRE at midnight   unless varied or discharged by this court at an earlier date.

ANY BREACH OF THIS ORDER IS AN OFFENCE contrary to s. 5(5) Protection from Harassment Act 1997.

Signed etc.

_____   _____

Justices Clerk   Chairman of the Bench

Copy to   1)   THE DEFENDANT PERSONALLY
          2)   Chief Officer Roddenberry Police Station
          3)   Jadzia Dax

(II)   RODDENBERRY YOUTH COURT
       RESTRAINING ORDER

On

THE DEFENDANT Benjamin Sisko
was convicted by this court of 3 offences contrary to s. 2(1) Protection from
Harassment Act 1997 and the court made the following restraining order against the
defendant under the provisions of s. 5(1) Protection from Harassment Act 1997.

1)   THE DEFENDANT IS PROHIBITED from drinking alcohol in the areas known
as Voyager Road, Enterprise Crescent, Bajor Comprehensive School or Cardassia
Park. This prohibition will not apply when the defendant is within his own home at
No. 9 Voyager Road or is within another house on Voyager Road or Enterprise
Crescent by invitation from the occupants of that house.

2)   THE DEFENDANT IS PROHIBITED from gathering by himself or with others
in the grounds of Bajor Comprehensive School or Cardassia Park between the hours
of 8 p.m. — 6 a.m.

3)   THE DEFENDANT IS PROHIBITED from staying away from school during
normal school hours unless he is ill and at home or his attendance is excused in writing
by the headmaster of his school.

4)   THE DEFENDANT IS PROHIBITED from shouting at, swearing at or insulting
in any way any person in the public areas or the private gardens of Voyager Road, or
Enterprise Crescent.

THIS ORDER SHALL EXPIRE at midnight   unless varied or discharged
by this court at an earlier date.

ANY BREACH OF THIS ORDER IS AN OFFENCE contrary to s. 5(5) Protection
from Harassment Act 1997.

Signed etc.

_____   _____
       Justices Clerk   Chairman of the Bench

Copy to   1)   THE DEFENDANT PERSONALLY
          2)   The Defendant's Parents
          3)   Chief Officer Roddenberry Police Station
          4)   Roddenberry District Council Social Services Department
          5)   The Headmaster Bajor Comprehensive School

(III)   IN THE CROWN COURT AT RODDENBERRY
        RESTRAINING ORDER

On

THE DEFENDANT Jean-Luc Picard

having been convicted on indictment of an offence contrary to s. 4(1) Protection from Harassment Act Her Honour Judge Kathryn Janeway made the following restraining order against the defendant under the provisions of s. 5(1) Protection from Harassment Act 1997.

1)   THE DEFENDANT IS PROHIBITED from making any contact of any type whatsoever either directly or indirectly with Deanna Troi.

2)   THE DEFENDANT IS PROHIBITED from making any contact of any type whatsoever either directly or indirectly with the parents of Deanna Troi namely Ian Troi and Luxwanna Troi.

3)   THE DEFENDANT IS PROHIBITED from taking any photographs or videos of Deanna Troi whether by long range lens or otherwise and is prohibited from employing or encouraging any person to take any such photographs or videos.

4)   THE DEFENDANT IS PROHIBITED from following the said Deanna Troi whether on foot or otherwise, and in particular is prohibited from visiting 'Quarks Bar' or '10 Forward Discotheque' whenever the said Deanna Troi is in either place.

5)   THE DEFENDANT IS PROHIBITED from being on or travelling down Voyager Gardens, and in addition is prohibited from visiting or waiting in the vicinity of the place of employment of the said Deanna Troi namely Romulan Assurance Services Ltd, DS9 Tower, Roddenberry.

THIS ORDER SHALL LAST until further order.

ANY BREACH OF THIS ORDER IS AN OFFENCE contrary to s. 5(5) Protection from Harassment Act 1997.

Signed etc.

Clerk of the Crown Court

Copy to   1)   THE DEFENDANT PERSONALLY
          2)   Chief Constable, Roddenberry Constabulary
          3)   The Governor HM Prison, Klingon Scrubbs
          4)   Deanna Troi

Index